RAGING RIVER

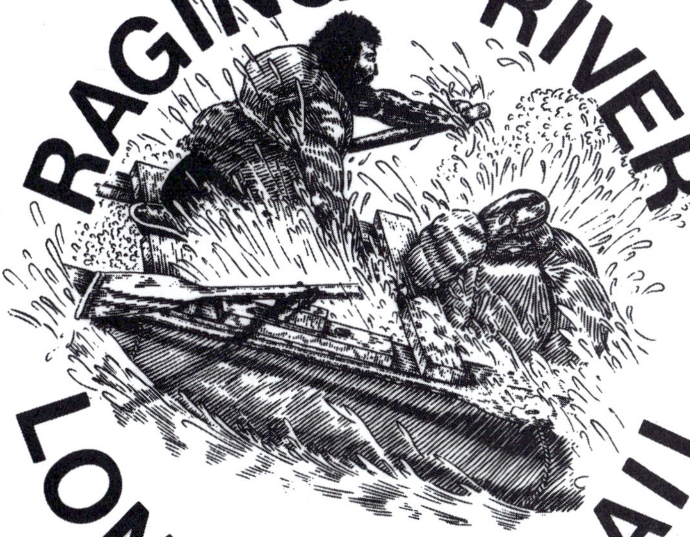

LONELY TRAIL

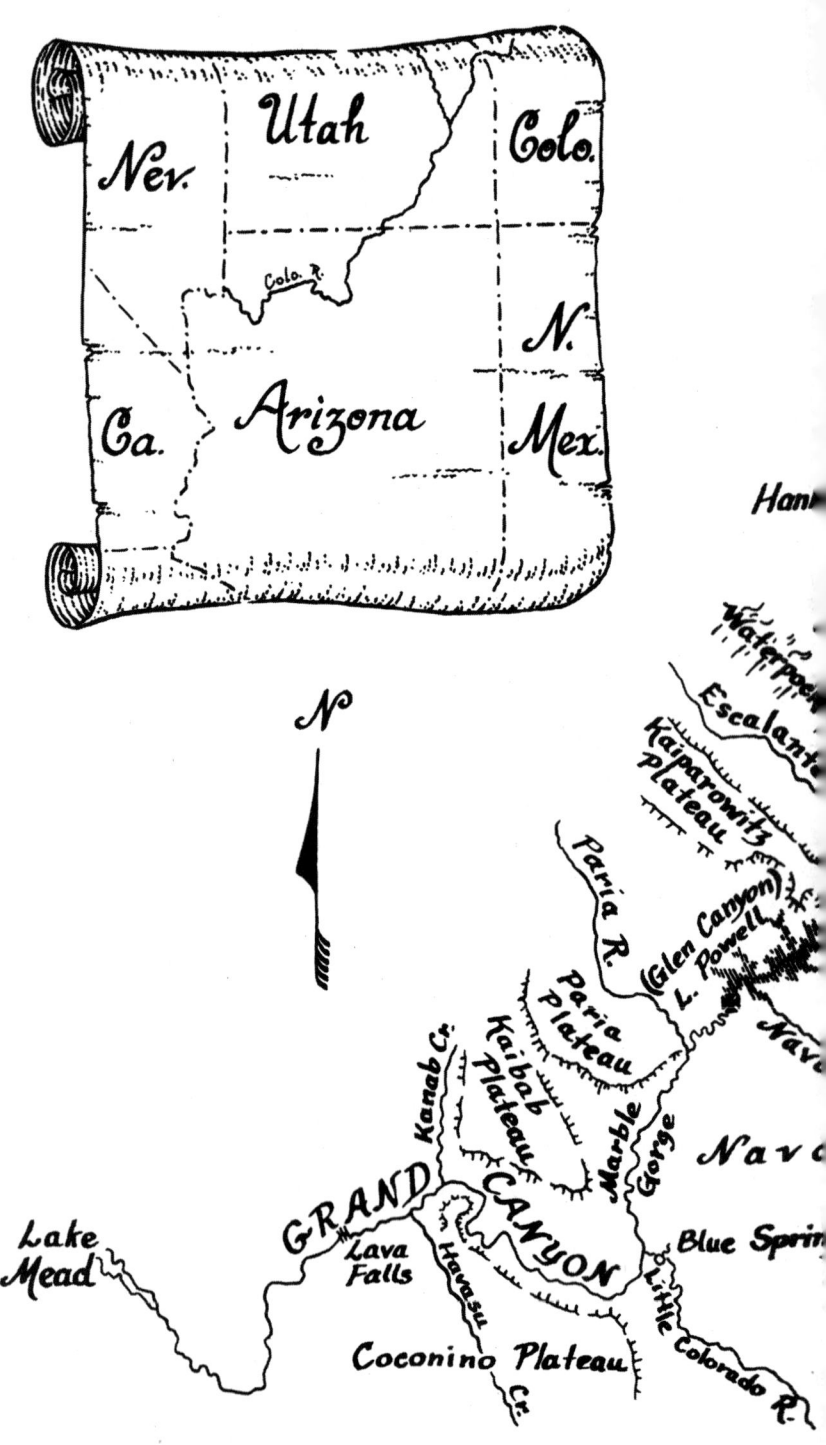

A Map of the Canyon Country Wherein Much of the Action Takes Place

Raging River Lonely Trail

Tails Told By the Campfire's Glow

The smoke of many campfires mingle to make this book. Campfires built in the deep, red canyons of Utah, by the big, roaring rapids of the mighty Colorado River, and high on the rising, blue mountains of Southern Arizona. Herein you will find nostalgia, lusty tales of adventure, and a bit of history. There is also sorrow over the passing of the old places and the old ways but winding throughout like a lazy delta stream are fantasy and whimsical humor.

Vaughn Short
Illustrated by Joanna Coleman

Copyright © 2014 Glen Canyon Natural History Association

All Rights Reserved
No portion of this book may be reproduced in whole or in part, by any means (with the exception of short quotes for the purpose of review), without permission of the publisher.

New Edition Designed by Christopher K. Eaton
Illustrated by Joanna Coleman
Cover Designed by Bronze Black

Printed in Canada by Friesens on 100% Post-Consumer Waste paper

Second Edition
10 9 8 7 6 5 4 3 2 1

ISBN 978-0-9622233-4-1

Originally published in 1978 by Two Horses Press

Glen Canyon Natural History Association is a non-profit cooperating association that supports and funds education, research, interpretation, and visitor services within the public lands on the Colorado Plateau. Working in partnership with Glen Canyon National Recreation Area, Rainbow Bridge National Monument, and Grand Staircase-Escalante National Monument, we promote and inspire the preservation and stewardship of cultural and natural resources. Net proceeds from the sale of this book will directly support interpretation, education, and research on your public lands.

Glen Canyon Natural History Association
PO Box 1835
Page, AZ 86040-1835
(877) GLEN-CYN
www.GlenCanyonNHA.org

The author gratefully acknowledges the "team"... Elaine who read the manuscript when it was very rough... Joanna who not only illustrated the book but took me by the hand and led me through the jungle of publishing... Louise and Carolyn who were always there whenever I yelled, "conference"... Angie who typed and proofread... and Alan who talked me out of calling the book, "Ralph."

Contents

Foreward 15
Preface 19
Prologue 21
"In the wilds of old Alaska" 23
The Ballad of the Smith-Corona Kid 26
"A dreamer lives in beauty and a dreamer lives in peace" 37
I've always been a dreamer 38
"He stood an Indian, strange, apart" 40
Two Horses 42
"They dream of a mighty boom and a quake" 43
Floyd's Void 44
"I toast you in my dream" 48
A Bit of Country 49
"High above in the cold night air I heard the stir of wind" 50
The Spirit of the Trail 51
"I shivered as I stoked my fire" 56
The Hour is Late 56
"Out of the south the hawk faced legions came" 59
Grand Canyon—The Discovery 1540 60
"What happened to those people down below" 62
Seldom Seen and His Macho Crew 63
"The Silver bells go jing-a-ling as the little people dance" 66
Elves Chasm 67
"On unhearing ears the words were talked" 69
Farewell To Rainbow 70
"Columbus was only the first tourist" 73
Those Old Ones 74
"I may not be like your other children" 76
A Boatman's Prayer 76
"...and Maggie smiled at me" 80
The Little Things 81
"The shadows are deep and the light is dim
where the wild water froths and flows" 82
The Ballad of Belle Zabor 83

"It's your own damn fault if you have no fun" 93
Really What the Hell? 94
"I gazed in the campfires glow" 97
My Soul 98
"On the side of the hill in old Jerome" 100
For Katie 100
"There's sandstone canyons in my dreams" 103
A Song of Glen 104
"So many things that you could tell" 107
Will Kelly's Grave 109
"Then his niche in life he found" 112
The Macho Boatman 112
"Drain down that stagnant pond" 115
Open the Gates 116
"What better place than a mountain top" 117
Musing on a Mountain 119
"I Thought of only you my dear" 123
Of You My Dear 124
"What are your thoughts, Kathy, my dear" 125
Kathy 126
"Those were the things that were whispered to me" 127
The Old Grand Gulch At Night 128
"On a lucky try at water low" 130
Lava Falls 130
"To really pass the test supreme" 132
The Ballad of Bare-Ass Bill 133
Epilogue 154

For the Green River Navy

Foreword

Vaughn Short was born on the summer solstice, 1923, in the southern Arizona mountain locality of Rucker Canyon; the middle child of three. Vaughn grew up working a series of no-account mining claims as his father searched for ways to support the family.

As an underage teenager, Vaughn went to work deep underground – and often under water – in Bisbee's infamous Copper Queen mine. He later said he should have been tattooed "Born to Dig," as he quickly broke every record for number of tons dug or cars filled by any previous mortal. Not knowing that many rumored records were merely mythical, he went on to break those too.

Short traded that dark, steamy, underground hell for a green, steamy, bullet-filled hades in Mindanao for much of World War II. With no training other than his own wits, he acted as a medic for much of the Pacific campaign, serving as doctor, friend, counselor, and scribe to his fellow soldiers.

After the war, he mined and farmed in southern Arizona. He married Louise in 1955, raising her two children and two of their own. The fact that he managed to have any spare time in those years is remarkable, but he did, and took up hiking in the nearby mountains when he could get away.

In 1961, Vaughn signed on for two adventures with Ken Sleight, a pack and river guide then on his way to becoming Canyon Country's most ardent defender – a home-grown environmentalist later immortalized as Seldom Seen Smith in Edward Abbey's *The Monkey Wrench Gang*. I say they were adventures because Ken's voyages were never tours. Things went wildly awry on a regular basis, leaving Ken, his clients, and crew to pull things back together and carry on. Vaughn, even before the end of the first trip – a mule-packing trip in the Escalante – had crossed over from client to crew. Two weeks later he was floating Glen Canyon as Sleight's right-hand man.

For nearly two decades, Short and Sleight trudged, packed, and floated the canyons and mesas each summer. At night around the campfires, Vaughn often read or recited poetry by Badger Clark, Robert Service, and others. Somewhere in there his own poems began to form and trickle out in the campfire smoke, unwritten and still taking shape, stored not on paper but in his mind.

After much prodding from friends, clients, and admirers in the mid-1970s, Vaughn began working on the original edition of this book. *Raging Rivers, Lonely Trails* became an instant classic on the rivers and trails of the Southwest. Vaughn's home-built, rough-metered cowboy poetry seemed to fit the place in a way that fancier, jazzed-up verbiage could not approach.

I first met Vaughn toward the end of the ninth poem in this book. As he and Sleight walked across the beach to leave the epic low-water Grand Canyon trip of 1977, I was the gangly, young boatman hiking in to take the extra boat on through with the infamous macho crew. We shook hands and smiled. When I saw Vaughn performing his poetry that fall at a river guides' meeting, he remembered me and we caught up. We bumped into one another on the river and at gatherings for decades afterward, becoming closer friends each time. At the annual Grand Canyon River Guides Training Seminar at Marble Canyon, Vaughn was always a hit, and was pronounced the Poet Lariat of Canyon Country.

When Ken eased out of the river business a few years later, Vaughn shifted his river operations to Sleight's long-time friends, the Quist family of Moki Mac Expeditions. He accompanied many of their trips for another decade or so during which he wrote his second book of poetry, *Two Worlds*. Finally, in 1991, I had the great treat of running a full trip with Vaughn – a long, slow-paced float through Desolation Canyon on the Green River of Utah. There in the Cottonwood and Box Elder groves along the shore, I finally got to hear Vaughn's tales and poetry in their native setting, amid the fire's flicker and wafts of juniper smoke. He spoke slowly, clearly, with an accent that could only have come from Rucker Canyon. His readings of journals of his early trips with Sleight, peppered with long perfectly-paced pauses, were side-splitting. He had no shortage of material, and often went on until everyone faded into the darkness. To call it a treat is not enough – it was and remains one of my greatest treasures.

With Vaughn's passing in 2010, his poetry was in danger of disappearing - clung to by a diminishing number of boatmen and guides with their dog-eared original volumes. So it is with great joy that we see Vaughn coming back into print for future generations.

But take this caveat: it will not read properly indoors. Take the book outside, into a slickrock canyon or along a rapid river. Wait until dark. Light a fire. Wait until folks gather after dinner and the clamor of camp has subsided. Allow people to hear the silence for a while. Then, when the time is right, read the poems aloud: slowly, clearly, with the hint of a desert drawl. Let the firelight do its magic. Repeat as necessary.

Brad Dimock
Tapeats Creek, April 2013

Raging River, Lonely Trail

Preface

This book is a collection of verse I have recited for friends around campfires – campfires built in remote canyons, by far mountain trails, or on the banks of whitewater rivers. The book was really never written, not in the sense of a disciplined writer sitting down and applying himself. It just happened. The poetry is something I did to entertain the people at night after I had cleaned up the supper pots and pans. Some of these poems were recited around many campfires before they were ever put on paper. For this reason they may vary a bit from tapes that people have recorded.

These verses are products of the backcountry and were not intended for the parlor. I've always had misgivings about how they might appear on the printed page. They are meant to be told aloud, and are tailored for my "Texas-once-removed" drawl. In the beginning I had no intentions of writing a book of poetry. After considerable prodding from insistent friends I decided, "What the heck! Why not give it a whirl?" At first I thought about a big rewrite; a massive smooth-up job. Then I changed my mind. Now, no one knows better than I that the great backdrop of the wilderness, the exhilaration of a day on the rapids, the friendly flames of the campfires, they've all helped to carry my poems. These verses were born on the river and the trail. They are meant for the river and the trail. Let them stand unpolished and unchanged, on whatever merits they may possess. Before each poem I've added a bit of explanation as to its origin, where it was written, or maybe something of my mood at the time.

Vaughn Short

Prologue

Come – Let me tell a tale.
Let me speak to you
Of raging river – lonely trail
Of misty mountain rising blue.

Of whispering pine on skyline crest,
Campfire casting warming glow
Of canyon wall with eagles nest
River flowing far below –

From down a ridge a poor will's call
Of hazy buttes in barren land,
Snow fed stream o'er waterfall
Of twisted tree and blowing sand.

Should these fumbling writings here
Take you far from street and town
Bring back some memory that's dear
Then I'm pleased I set them down.

Raging River, Lonely Trail

"In the wilds of old Alaska"

In the beginning I had no poems. Around the smoky campfires at night I would tell tales. Some of them were true tales, some were tall tales, and some were tales of the old times. If I recited any poetry it would be from one of the great outdoor poets—poets like Badger Clark, Robert Service, or the ill-fated wanderer, Everett Ruess. Somehow poetry spoken aloud seems to fit the outdoor scene.

I have always liked to rhyme words. When I was small, grammar school size, I had a burning desire to be a poet. For one spring and maybe awhile into summer, I became a poetry mill and really ground it out. With much smudge and erasing, never having been a tidy one, I filled the lines of many a nickel tablet. The kind that had the red covers with the Indian chief in full headdress upon them. It was super-patriotic, red-blooded American, flag waving, stand up and cheer writing. My heroes always waxed triumphant. Looking back, for a little tyke, it was great stuff. I often wonder when and where I lost that special touch.

Now summer is a nice season, especially when you are a kid and out of school, but it doesn't carry the romance of spring. Maybe that's why I decided against the life of a poet and turned to more manly doings. Every boy in our ranch community wanted to be a trapper in the White Mountains and then there was always the glamour of cowboying, but the thing that really gripped my fancy was to pioneer in Alaska. We had an Atlas. I think it had been ordered from the old *Literary Digest* magazine. The map of Alaska Territory was colored green. I just about wore that page out.

I tried to make a clean break with that sissy poetry stuff but somehow it was very difficult to rip up something I had worked so hard over and had once been so proud of. You leave something of yourself in a poem. It is a very personal thing. After some pondering, the way to go seemed a decent burial. I rolled it all into tight rolls and stuffed it into cans. Into yellow, K. C. brand baking powder containers that were so plentiful back in the days before store bought bread. With their tin, push on tops, they made snug little coffins. At a secret, secluded spot on the old homestead I dug the graves all in a row, did the ashes to ashes and dust to dust bit and consigned my poetry forever to the ravages of time.

Years passed, children became grownups, droughts came and went, wars were fought and I kept that old poetic urge well bottled up. Oh, I read a lot of poetry, memorized a lot, even recited a bit, but my composing days seemed over. One night it all came bubbling out. I was hiking in Grand Gulch in remote southeastern Utah. Darkness wasn't far off when I climbed from my truck that I had parked on the rim and shouldered my pack. It's always exhilarating to be out in the wilderness. To be alone deep in the back country, out doing your own thing, it's a big turn on. Two miles later I was still in high spirits when I reached the dark canyon bottom and passed through that narrow slot that divides the upper gulch from the lower.

Around the first bend and I was in moonlight, moonlight at its glorious best. Moonlight that would bathe the canyon in day-like atmosphere and then disappear at the next bend, leaving me stumbling through the darkness. Moonlight that would next appear high on the wall, and then creep downward until the canyon bottom took on an unreal, eerie appearance. It was a wild, wild night. One of the most beautiful I have ever hiked. Soon the spirits of the ancient cliff dwellers were all about. Grand Gulch abounds in the crumbling dwellings of the old ones. With the spirits of by-gones I get along fabulously. We have no communication problem. I suppose it has some thing to do with the Irish genes inherited from my mother. Now I can speak right out loud to a spirit. If it should care to answer back it will plant a little thought in my head and suddenly I will find it there. I don't think this works for everyone. As my kids would say, "You've got to be a little dingey!" Sometimes it becomes a bit difficult to separate my true thoughts from those of the long departed, therefore, I can't truthfully say who started this resurgence to poetry. Maybe it was me, maybe them, but suddenly I was mumbling in rhyme. Crude unpolished verse it was, but nevertheless I was rhyming and my first ballad was born.

I often take back country trips with Ken Sleight, a long time friend and veteran river and trail guide. At night I would recite to his groups around the campfires and over the years my collection of material expanded. Most of my tales in rhyme were based in the canyon country of Utah or the mountains of Arizona. This was natural, this was my stomping grounds, but I still had this old, latent dream of the polar regions. Maybe that's what brought about my one and only Alaskan ballad or perhaps because an acquaintance started talking about moving north. That stirred old memories. I too had once dreamed of an Alaskan cabin deep in the wilderness. Discussing her plans one day this girl with sourdough longings mentioned that when she made her move she would have to buy a gun because of the bears. Now I happened to recall that stuck up in the rafters of my humble abode was a rifle, a relic of a by-gone war. I leaned the ladder against the house and crawled through the eaves, found the old gun in its nest of cobwebs and presented it to my friend with best wishes.

This future denizen of the northern wilds likes to bang and clang around. She industriously set about chipping the rust away, even uncovered the name of the manufacturer which turned out to be a well-known typewriter company that had tooled over in war time. After liberal splashings and soakings with oil, the gun even looked shootable. Those old military rifles were made wooded to the end of the barrel but sometime years back, in a moment of ambition, I had taken a hand saw and given it one of those fast, three minute, economy, money saving, sporterizing jobs. It didn't look too bad.

If you are the proud new owner of a customized, Smith Corona, sporting rifle you naturally want to try it out. With a great display of artistic talent, this girl drew a bear on a big piece of cardboard, a real mean looking devil, mostly tooth and claw. We took this to some nearby mountains and nailed it to a blackjack oak tree. I explained to her why you put your arm, not your leg, through the sling, showed her which end of the cartridge went in first and said, "Okay, Kid, have at it." She stepped back and peppered that target but good. Shot a pattern that would have been the envy of any advocate of the sawed-off shotgun. 'I'm ready," she said, "Bring on your bear!"

I'm a great admirer of courage, even the kind that makes you shake your head a bit. I'm sure her brave stance and unwavering confidence, all our talk about guns, bears, and Alaska had something to do with this ballad of the North. Most of my writings are created on the scene. I am thankful that I was many miles away when I wrote this one.

THE BALLAD OF THE SMITH-CORONA KID

Oh mothers bed the wee ones down
Then turn your dainty ear
For this tale of blood and carnage
Is not for you to hear.

It is a tale of terror
The likes never heard before
A tale of horror and mayhem
Of mangled guts and gore.

In the wilds of old Alaska
Where the ferocious grizzly prowls
Where the moose browse in the thickets
And the restless grey wolf howls.

Where dangers there are many
Where lurking menaces lay hid
There dwelt a mighty hunter
Called The Smith-Corona Kid.

There in wooded hummock green
Known to only a fearful few
A sage old brownie once dug a den
Where he slept the winter through.

When the deep snow began to yield
To the melting winds of spring
The hungry bruin tunneled out
Impatient to do his thing.

He was a wise old warrior
And he ruled a vast terrain
Where he viciously fought all comers
Who challenged his domain.

So he set out that early spring
To build up his wind and strength.
To pounce on the tasty marmot
To fish the streams at length.

But as the summer slowly passed
And he grew fat and sleek
He felt a longing deep within
And he knew what he must seek.

Fresh scarred from mating battles fought
Weary from many bloody rows.
Short tempered and with impatience fraught
And weakened from the sows.

He hungered not for berries sweet
Or wiggly grubs to munch,
His craving was for dripping meat
And good white bones to crunch.

He needed bad a super meal
A meal of blood and flesh.
No stinking carrion would do.
It must be warm and fresh.

By instinct he slowly turned
Toward where Smith-Corona dwelled
For there in recent weeks
A human he had smelled.

And as the old bear ambled on
Sniffing—grumbling—coughing
This deadly kid was seeking him,
There was battle in the offing.

For Smith-Corona had woke that morn
Her larder she did scan.
She badly needed bear fat
With which to grease her pan.

She took her gun from off the wall,
Ran the ramrod through the bore,
Thought of the fat an old bear had
And declared herself at war.

She set her course beyond a lake
Out through the forest green
Where in the bogs in recent weeks
Huge bear tracks had been seen.

She sniffed the little breezes
That wafted down the hill
And her eyes were darting to and fro
Searching for the kill.

And if she ever spotted him
Caught a glimpse of that old bear
She'd pop some lead into his hide
And bag him fair and square.

The Kid paused on a wooded crest
To give herself a blow
But her eyes and ears were open
She sensed bruin down below.

Then suddenly in the morning breeze
Brownie smelled the human taint
He stealthily started to circle 'round
While Smith looked where he ain't.

Oh little did this hunter guess
It never crossed her mind
That this old bear had called her hand
And was closing in behind.

But heed you well old grumbling bear
As to what may be your lot
For you're stalking the Smith-Corona Kid
Who's never missed a shot.

And heed you also Kid so bold
As you so daringly advance
If that old bear ever gets a hold
Then you haven't got a chance.

Behind her back she heard a noise
The snapping of a twig!
She wheeled about to take a look
And Smitty's eyes got big.

In record time she raised her gun
Six loud times the roar
But that old bear kept coming on
Reeking blood and gore.

There upon that alder slope
Rose the smell of powder burned
And sweet-sick stench of fresh bled blood
Where tide of battle quickly turned.

Teeth gleaming white and claws on high
The bear charged into the fray
With one swipe of mighty paw
He knocked her gun away.

Raging River, Lonely Trail

Run, Smith-Corona, run!
It's time you turned and fled
But she gamely grabbed her gun back up
And swung it round her head.

There they fought with no holds barred
Where everything is fair
Now the advantage swings Smitty's way
And now back to the bear.

Alder bushes swayed and snapped
As they both fought for the kill
And soon there was a gaping scar
On the side of that old hill.

And mingled there was roar with swear
As they locked in deadly strife
And toe to toe, blow for blow
They battled for their life.

Oh glory to that raging beast.
Who would not cease to fight
And glory to that gallant girl,
Brave, but not too bright.

There upon that ravaged slope
It was settled once for all.
So bravely was the battle fought
'Twas a shame one had to fall.

In the lodges of the Athabascan
As they pass the long cold night
They tell of scar on hill afar
And a wild and bloody fight.

And slowly o'er that great cold land
A whispered tale leaks out
So varied were the stories told
They left us all in doubt.

Pale gleam the polar stars
In the dead of arctic night
Where like ghost of mystic mountain
Old Denali rises white.

Most buried in the pale blue snow
Near frozen lake by rocky bar
A lonesome cabin nestles low
In valley deep and far.

So we seek this cabin out
In this cold and icy hell
For we have a need to know
If Smitty's alive and well.

For we've heard this awful rumor
The one that's filtered out
Of how a valiant girl was killed
In cruel and bloody bout.

"Oh, no!," we cried. "It can't be so.
Not our pal and friend.
Rumbling in some old bears gut
That's no way to meet your end."

So we made a solemn vow
No matter what the odds might be
We'd venture forth to this frigid north
To see what we could see.

So far across that frozen land
We snowshoed and broke trail
Until we huddle before this hut
Heartsick and woefully pale.

Now we stand with heads hung low
Before that rough hewn door
And steel ourselves for instant grief
For what may be in store.

Raging River, Lonely Trail

Will everything ship-shape stand
Although she may no longer be on the scene
Or maybe it'll be in great disarray
From some marauding wolverine.

But still there glimmers a faint far hope
Through all our bleak despair.
Please—when we peek inside that room,
Let that wayward kid be there.

So we summon our courage up
And pray to him above,
Slowly pull on the old latch string
And give that door a shove.

By the rosy glow of a Yukon stove
Sits Smitty full of life
Picking bear meat from out her teeth
With the point of her skinning knife.

And proudly there upon the wall
Hangs her trusty hunting piece
Her old faithful Smith-Corona
In its coating of bear grease.

There's bear grease in her shining hair
To make her look her best
Bear grease on her body smeared
For the rattle in her chest.

Around her neck a string of beads
Made from teeth and claws.
Suspended from a ceiling beam
A hunk of bear meat thaws.

There's bear grease mixed within her bread
Her bear oil lamp burns bright
As she sits there on her bear skin rug
In that long cold arctic night.

No sooner had I finished this ballad when a great clamor of protest went up among my faithful fans (all seven of them). Seems bears are jolly old clowns. They make great cartoon characters. Little kiddies have cute stuffed teddy bears to cuddle. How dare I make one of these lovable old oafs into a bad guy and a loser. In hand-to-hand combat with a mere human, the bear has to be the good guy. No way was my public going to let me get away with a girl beating a poor old bruin to death with a rifle. I yielded to the heat, braced myself for the wrath of women's lib and gave brother bear a second chance. There are far more women than bears in this old world. Surely one is expendable. This was the best I could do for the old grubeater, the burden fell squarely back upon his shoulders. In rhyming, the poet is only the vehicle. He has little control over the direction a poem will take. Let's back up to where the door swings open and this is the new version. Better luck this go round, Brownie.

Oh Dear God! It's so!
Smith-Corona isn't there.
Only silence fills that hut.
So bleak—So cold—so bare.

The emptiness of this silent room
A heart-breaking tale does tell
Dazed we stand in disbelief
Our hopes all shot to hell.

Then reeling from this staggering blow
Our reason comes unhinged
Loud we scream our fury out,
"This kid must be avenged!"

With tear-streaked cheeks we stand
And we swear by all that's bad
That never again will rest be ours
'Till vengeance we have had.

So we probe the frozen banks
For somewhere here we know
Curled into a slumbering ball
A bear sleeps down below.

Raging River, Lonely Trail

Then from o'er a rounded hill
Comes a loud triumphant whoop.
Fast we scurry to the spot
And gather in a group.

Somewhere beneath that high-piled snow
Comes a cry of bleak despair
We gather tools and all pitch in.
This has to be our bear.

The wind it blew in icy burst
Straight down from the pole
As we chipped and shoveled and cursed
And slowly dug a hole.

Then with a crack the crust breaks through
And we almost tumble in
As sickening stench comes reeking out
Of that foul and fetid den.

With light we probe the inky depths
And prepare ourselves to shoot.
Outlined there upon the floor
Lies that huge ferocious brute.

We gasp for breath—our eyes bug out
From the terrible sight we saw.
It seemed unreal—It couldn't be so
Not this much tooth and claw!

Scattered about upon the floor
Much to our grief and dismay
'Mid tattered bits of red bandana
Some tufts of gray hair lay.

Once again the rage sets in
And we scream out our wrath and ire
But something in that scene within
Makes us hold our fire.

Something about that awesome beast
Just doesn't seem quite right.
He should be curled in slumber deep
Through this long cold winter night.

Instead he rolls with moan and groan
Jerks and jumps in agony.
That this old brownie is in distress
It's very plain to see.

You can tell this old bear knows
His days are numbered now.
He won't come forth this spring
To battle for the sow.

He's resigned to fate, this grizzled one
Even though it galls and rubs.
Some other bear will have the fun
And father all the cubs.

Loud he cries in whimpering pain
There's no way that he can rest
For there's a stubborn lump within his gut
That refuses to digest.

It's true that Smitty had fallen
Gone down in blood and gore
But she'd only lost the skirmish
She still was waging war.

We did not shoot that suffering brute
Not even for Smith-Corona's sake
For we plainly saw that before spring thaw
He'd die of belly ache.

So we turn our backs on old Denali
Who rises like a pale, white ghost.
Kill the last of our booze and on snowshoes
Set out for the faraway coast.

Raging River, Lonely Trail

A haven at last from wintery blast
In boozy bar in settlement town
We cringe and careen from that terrible scene
And our sorrows try to drown.

Now maybe there's a moral
To this tale of grief and woe
Or maybe there's a warning,
I'm sure that I don't know.

But if I was a mean old bear
I'd take this for an omen
If I hankered for taste of human flesh
I'd make sure it wasn't woman.

"A dreamer lives in beauty and a dreamer lives in peace"

I've always been a dreamer. I've never cared too much about serious thought, the kind where you have to furrow the brow and tax the brain. The drifty, dreamy kind of thinking that's my style—the lazy man's way of thinking. As a boy I saw little of the outside, just a trip to town before Christmas and maybe a couple of times during the summer. Other than those thirty mile adventures into the unknown, my world was restricted to the community. I read a lot, thought a lot, and dreamed a lot.

Occasionally on clear, cold winter mornings you could hear, faint and far away, the whistle of a train passing the little wayside station of Apache. To me, this was a happening. It was really a thrill. To a town kid it would have meant nothing. Apache was only twenty miles away, but there was a big blue mountain in between. Trains were another world. How I thrilled to that lonesome, drawn-out whistle.

When I was up a grade or two in school, we had our first radio. It hooked up to a large assortment of batteries and a long aerial. If atmospheric conditions were right, it could be heard after dark. Otherwise it was only scratching, popping, and feeble squawking. The stations that we received were San Antonio, Del Rio, Denver, Salt

Lake, and Hollywood. This opened up vast new horizons. There was a big unknown world out there, somewhere. A big unknown world to dream about, and dream I did.

I went to work in the copper mines as a teenager. It was hard, dangerous work, but it had its compensations. Standing on rubble, watching the heavy drill bite into the rock face, I was truly alone, cloaked in anonymity by the roar of the big pneumatic drill and the fog of its swirling exhaust. There I could laugh, shout, sing, and think outlandish thoughts. All were drowned instantly and forever in the all-encompassing din. For one who liked to dream, it wasn't bad. I could even dream right out loud, and still they were my secrets. Halfway 'round the world, and at war, I continued to dream, but now I dreamed of peace and home. Dreaming's always been my thing.

I've Always Been a Dreamer

I've always been a dreamer and I suppose I always will
But I really don't believe that it's so bad
When I think about the beauty and I think about the thrill
Of all those good times dreaming that I've had.

I've climbed the highest mountains on the face of this
  old world
And I've revelled in the vistas from their crest.
The beauties of the valleys before me lay unfurled,
Though these were only dreams, maybe dreams are best.

I've always been a dreamer and I've dreamed my life away
But I really wouldn't change it if I could.
I've gathered me no fortune as I've lived from day to day,
For I really don't believe a dreamer should.

I've dreamed with pleasure of many girls who've marched
  in life's parade
And my heart beat loud in love to quite a few.
The moments they were tender as a whole new life we made
But these were only dreams and they really never knew.

I've always been a dreamer and I've dreamed down through the years.
In dreams there isn't much I haven't done
But it's saved me lots of heartaches and it's saved me lots of tears.
I've seen my share of beauty and I've had my share of fun.

But I've never dreamed of glory and I've never dreamed of fame.
The very thought of money leaves me cold.
Let the hero have the lime light—May he revel in the same.
Let the mizer have his horde of gleaming gold.

For a dreamer lives in beauty and a dreamer lives in peace.
His little niche in life it may be small.
But he doesn't need a Midas touch or sheep with golden fleece,
For his modest home in dreamland tops them all.

Raging River, Lonely Trail

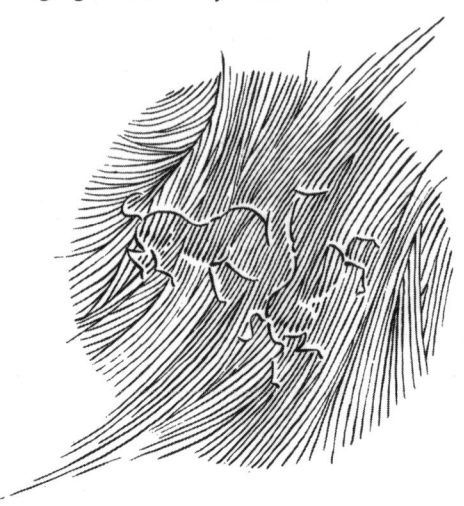

"He stood an Indian, strange, apart"

It was raining like hell down in San Juan County, Utah. In October the weather should have been better. Someone upstairs was playing a big joke. This was supposed to be desert country. There were five in our group, all old friends. We were hanging around Cedar Mesa waiting for a break in the weather. Grand Gulch was our ultimate destination, but with the rains, a trek through the Gulch wasn't too hot an idea. We were committed to go, however.

Edna Fridley was already in the Gulch. She had gone down before the storm began. We had to go down and see about Edna. Not once did we consider doing otherwise.

We camped for the night in the old corral on Kane Creek. Next day it looked as though the water was down enough to wade our pack animals through, so we took off.

Jan Tibbetts and Virginia Kavanaugh, the two girls in our group, started down first. They dutifully stopped and recorded their names in the B. L. M. (Bureau of Land Management) register at the trail head. After we finished packing the animals, Ken Sleight and I came next. With a rather disdainful glance at the trail signs, we passed the register by. Bringing up the rear of our caravan was Tad Nichols. Tad has to be classified as an authentic "old timer" in the red rock country. He was exploring it long before the asphalt came. Now Tad wasn't about to go down that canyon without letting the proper people know. He affixed his name to the register and added, "Down the canyon with Ken Sleight and two horses." Then as an afterthought he wrote, "and Vaughn Short."

Vaughn Short

This trek into Grand Gulch ultimately turned out to be a much-talked-about affair. It's been good for a lot of campfire conversation. We never did get our pack animals beyond the junction of Kane Creek and the Gulch. There we made camp under the overhangs and the rains came down. Edna was found down below and brought back to camp. Then we sat under the cliffs and watched the waterfalls spill over the top. In the days to come, we saw a lot of water rushing by on its way to the San Juan River. One night an especially big flood came rumbling down, roaring like a speeding freight train. To continue down through the Gulch was impossible, to return to the trail head was very risky, so we decided to sit it out. Late one evening, a raven appeared in the canyon and flew about. Could this be an omen, we wondered? Next morning the sun broke through and the creek was down. We wasted no time in packing out. Ken and I stopped at the register we had ignored on our way in, just snooping to see what the people might have written. He saw my name listed after the two horses and it delighted him no end.

Next spring, we were in Forgotten Canyon, a drainage off the old Glen Canyon. Ken, Jan Pilling, and I had hiked beyond the rest of the group. I was showing them a plant that produced very astringent bulbs that Indians sometimes harvest. Ken took a great interest, and we soon had our knives out and were digging. This particular plant was a high yielder, and as our pile of roots grew, the hole went deeper and deeper into the sandy soil. Soon we had to stretch out on the ground to reach bottom. Jan was snapping pictures from all angles and things were getting a little ridiculous, including the conversation. About this time the story of the register over on Kane Creek came up. Ken still found this amusing. Now Jan Pilling was a new friend. I didn't want her thinking my social standing was somewhere below that of two rather nondescript pack horses. I reached far down into our hole and I came up with an idea. The Indians have a name for Barry Goldwater. As a fellow native Arizonan, wasn't I just as entitled to have one? "Look," I said, "Two Horses, that's my Indian name! When Tad wrote, 'Ken Sleight and Two Horses' in the register he was referring to me. He added the 'Vaughn Short' as an afterthought, just in case someone not in the know might wander by." The name, Two Horses, survived. I've received mail addressed to it. Strangers have knocked on the door looking for Two Horses.

You get the picture. It was early spring. We were in Forgotten Canyon digging bitter roots, and old Two Horses was literally dragged out of a hole in the ground. The following little poem resulted.

Two Horses

In the forgotten canyon of the bitter root,
T'was the moon when the tree buds swell
A noble red man came to be
Of his birth this tale will tell.

Born not of woman, born not of love,
From a hole in the ground he came,
He announced in the paleface tongue,
"Two Horses is my name!"

He never knew the warm brown breast,
No cradle board, no childhood games.
He never rode the warpath trail.
He counts no coups among his claims.

He stood an Indian, strange, apart,
No tribal allegiance which to swear,
No copper skin, no regal stance,
No braids of long black hair.

No pipe of peace, no wampum belt,
No brothers red at his council fires,
No comely squaws to bid his will,
Or tend to his desires.

Among the ancients, grey and old,
Steeped in wisdom, long on pride,
In deepest sleep the visions come
To show them how to lead and guide.

Though of many winters and many springs
Two Horses, incredible Indian of numerous flaws,
Gathers no wisdom in his sleep
For he dreams at night of young white squaws.

"The dream of a mighty boom and quake"

Around the driftwood campfires along the Colorado River, Glen Canyon Dam gets a lot of discussion. It's probably the number two topic among the boatmen. (Naturally the ladies hold down first spot.) Any boatman worth his salt can tell you the location of Dominy Falls, that huge rapid that exists only in wishful thinking. It is formed by the rubble of a demolished Glen Canyon Dam. You see, not everyone is madly in love with the concrete barrier that forms Lake Powell. Now it can't be denied that the dam still stands firm and staunch, but people have the right to dream, so the talk goes on. This rebellious thinking helps a lot to relieve frustrations as the bureaucratic red tape piles ever higher upon the free spirited river boating people.

Talk of blowing the dam is a fun game not unlike Monopoly. A person can become a millionaire many times over in a lifetime of playing Monopoly and still have patches on his jeans. So it is with the dam. It is a fascinating subject, however, and it occupies some very keen minds.

Back during the construction of the dam, the opposition didn't fare too well. Some of the boatmen down in Glen cursed and pawed the sand a bit, but actually the Bureau of Reclamation had very smooth sailing. It was headed by Floyd Dominy, who was a very capable director. He had the weight of his bureaucracy behind him, and he used it to his advantage. The politicians in the states involved stood solidly for the project. The government had plenty of slick paper and colored ink to pour forth its propaganda. To the uninformed, it seemed that before the dam, Glen Canyon could be enjoyed only by the very rich. In actuality, nowhere else in the Colorado River canyons could the water be negotiated with greater ease or with such modest equipment. Commercial trips were a real bargain. Even during the heavy trip demands of the final season, you could still get a trip for a hundred bucks (a little more or less depending on the outfitter). Rainbow Bridge in those days was a moving experience, a true monument to solitude.

With a trace of satire, the poem, "Floyd's Void," was written as a rebuttal to Bureau propaganda, and in protest of the inundation of Glen, the most tranquil and beautiful canyon anywhere.

The old Glen Canyon was full of treasures aside from its green shorelines and towering red cliffs. It contained a wealth of archaeological sites. The ancient Moqui had dwelt within its walls and the cliff houses and writings were numerous. In the poem that follows are a few place names. Gregory Natural Bridge, Hidden Passage, Dungeon Canyon, and Music Temple get a mention. These represent only a few of many outstanding attractions covered by the water, muck, and gook of Lake Powell.

Floyd's Void

There's a breed of men who sit at their desks
And they like their water tame,
They like to damn the rivers up,
    Then give the lakes a name
        They do
    Then give the lakes a name.

So give three cheers for the Bureau boys
And a special rah for Floyd.
He built his dam and he built it well
And then he said, "In spite of hell,
    I'm going to fill that void
        I am
    I'm going to fill that void."

Now within this void, created by Floyd,
Was a special thing or two,
Reserved for the sight of the filthy rich
    And a very greedy few
        They were
    A very greedy few.

So give three cheers for the Bureau boys
And a special rah for Floyd.
For Floyd did say, "I'll change this plan,
  I'll open it up for the common man
      I will
  I'll open it up for the common man."

"What value the trees? What value the grasses,
Compared to the rights of the down-trodden masses?"
Floyd said, "I'll make it so easy,
I'll make it so simple,
They can all speed their boats over Music Temple
      How about that?
  Speed right over the top of Music Temple!"

So give three cheers for the Bureau boys
And a special rah for Floyd,
For now we know beneath the blue
  Is a revered spot once seen by few
      How sad
  Before Floyd's void seen only by few.

To see the Rainbow—aloof—remote—
You had to hike or you had to float.
Denied it was to that jolly old chap
By his houseboat rail in his yachting cap
      Oh my!
  Poor old chap in his yachting cap.

So give three cheers for the Bureau boys
And a special rah for Floyd.
Floyd said, "We'll put the water there
For this deserving old man in his easy chair,

For he's entitled to his just share
He is
He's entitled to his just share."

If one should insist on making a list
Of the many grandeurs there—
There were Gregory, Dungeon, Hidden Passage
And many more I swear
Oh Yes!
There were many more I swear.

So give three cheers for the Bureau boys
And a special rah for Floyd.
He buried them all deep under his lake
But he did it for the people's sake
He did
He did it for the people's sake.

For the power hungry man with the dollar sign eyes,
Who lights up the neon in the evening skies,
For the poor down-trodden in his speeding boat,
For the jolly old chap in his yachting cap
Who had no water to float
Poor guy
He had no water to float.

So give three cheers for the Bureau boys
And a special rah for Floyd.
Though he buried the Moqui and he shortened the wall,
He did it for the good of all
He did
He did it for the good of all!

But there's a breed of men both hardy and free
Who lie at night on the lonely bars
And there beneath the glittering stars
They dream of TNT
They do
They dream of TNT.

So give three cheers for the Bureau boys
And a special rah for Floyd.
He built his dam and though he built it well,
These dreamers swear in spite of hell
    They're going to void Floyd's void
        They are
    They're going to void Floyd's void.

They dream of a mighty boom and a quake.
They dream of a swirl in a vanishing lake.
They dream of a river wild and free,
    Freed from its shackles by TNT
        Sweet bliss
    Freed from its shackles by TNT.

Now! Let's have three cheers for the boys on the bars
Who dream their dreams 'neath the glittering stars.
Who dream of a wild and a wonderful treat—
A house boat running Dominy Falls at a million second feet
        Ah yes
A house boat running Dominy Fails at a million second feet!

"I toast you in my dream"

In the little mining town of Lowell, Arizona, I once had a boarding house room on the top floor of an old, two-story, frame building. The ground floor was occupied by a small cafe and it had a jukebox. Upstairs was a railed porch that overlooked an asphalt plaza. When I was working the day shift, I often spent my evenings sitting on the porch. From my vantage I could see three saloons located more or less catty-cornered from one another. Periodically, a bar door would fly open and an over-lubricated customer would be flung out onto the pavement. After experiencing the same fate at all three establishments, this bruised and battered partaker of the spirits would usually end up in the cafe below. There he found plenty of sympathetic company, for it was the unofficial soberingup-place of most of the town drunks, both the occasionals and the regulars.

In keeping with the atmosphere, the cafe served the strongest coffee and had the saddest music on the jukebox. If there were any happy selections they didn't earn many nickels. The volume vibrated the whole upstairs. When I would get home off swing-shift, at midnight, the revelry (if revelry it was) would be in full sway. Many a night I tried to go to sleep with: Pins and Needles, Born to Lose, Low and Lonely, or some other one of the old goodies blaring through the floor. I became well versed in country music—"hillbilly music" we called it back then. It was far different from the old western ballads I had heard on the ranch as a youngster. Those we called "cowboy music."

Country music has changed over the years, but it still sticks to rather basic formulas. I like music, most any music, however I'm not the least bit musical. When I sing, my tunes all sound the same.

I've often thought if I could only sing and plunk on the guitar a bit, then I'd have no problem writing country songs. Fooling around one day I thought I'd try my hand at some lyrics. I took a tried and proven theme—love, broken love, and drowning the sorrows. I jotted down the following verses.

A BIT OF COUNTRY

Cool mountains rise when I close my eyes
And I drift away and dream,
To where a songbird flies through cloudless skies
And willows shade a stream.

There on the sand of this dream world land,
By the banks of this mountain stream,
On the finger of your hand I place a band
And kiss you in my dream.

My heart feels good, the way it should
When it beats loud with love
And if I only could, like the songbird would,
I'd rise up and soar above.

But your lips grow cold to my kisses bold
And my joy is turned to pain.
Though that ring of gold says you're mine to hold,
Your eyes show your disdain.

So I wake next morn' to a world forlorn,
In a lonely bed and sigh
And my heart is torn as I recall your scorn,
And I lay back down and cry.

Now when I close my eyes, bleak mountains rise
As I drift away and dream.
No songbird flies through the dreary skies
And the willows lay dead by the stream.

On the sterile sand of this nightmare land
By the banks of the dried up stream,
I look at the brand of the bottle in my hand
And I toast you in my dream.

Raging River, Lonely Trail

"High above in the cold night air I heard the stir of wind"

One of the mysteries of the canyon country is the disappearance of the boy, painter and poet, Everett Ruess. He wrote beautifully of this area, with a great sensitivity and a genuine love. He tramped over it extensively, living a life as simple as the native Indian. His dress was patterned after theirs. He wore the Navajo hat and turquoise jewelry. The Indians accepted him as though he was one of their own.

Like a waft of smoke from his last campfire, Everett vanished without a trace. In a side canyon of the Escalante River, his pack burros were found.

Ken Sleight and I read everything we could find written by Everett, and about the searches made for him after he so mysteriously disappeared. In our early hiking days together, one of our goals was to visit the lonely canyon where Everett's last camp was believed to have been. Perhaps we could locate that elusive clue that had evaded others. This was why we walked the edge of a straight-walled canyon one sub-zero evening, desperately searching for a way down. We had trudged for hours through sand, sage, and slickrock. Spending a night on the open desert wasn't an inviting prospect. In the canyon below there was wood, water, and sheltering walls. In those days, there were no beaten paths in the Escalante Canyons. Information was scanty and often unreliable. It was an explorer's paradise, a real challenge to the backpacker.

Just before dark we found that hoped for break in the wall that let us clamber down. We were in "Everett Ruess country". This was the same route he had used to gain entry. Here his animals had been found. Perhaps at this very spot he had made his last camp. He was foremost in our thoughts and conversation as we raced the darkness to prepare our meal. We had camped many times in similar canyons but this spot was special. The presence of the vanished lad seemed to hover here. The following is the simple little story of our camp that night.

THE SPIRIT OF THE TRAIL

One night we camped 'neath a stained red wall
Where a trail wound down from the rim,
The snow lay about from a recent fall
And the light was fast fading and dim.

We chipped through the ice of a tiny stream
And collected our water there.
On our kindled fire we watched it steam
And the cold was everywherte.

We gathered wood for the morning fire.
Our breaths blew cold in the night.
We scurried about so we could retire
With the last of the waning light.

As stars o'er head began to glow,
We ate our meal with hurried pace,
Then on the ground our beds did throw,
A long cold night to face.

As I snuggled deep to warm myself,
I remembered my cup of tea
Setting on a sandstone ledge,
Just out of reach of me.

But the bed, it felt so snug and warm,
So biting cold the air,
I said to myself, "It'll do no harm.
I'll leave it setting there."

Raging River, Lonely Trail

Night closed in as I gazed at the sky.
The canyon grew still and dark.
Stars peek-a-booed as clouds drifted by
And the walls loomed sheer and stark.

Then a stranger came in a Navajo hat
Or maybe this I just dreamed.
By the dying coals of our fire he sat
And on his wrist three turquoise gleamed.

In his rough shod shoes and faded jeans,
I saw he was just a lad.
Weary from the trail he leans,
And his face was almost sad.

He seemed so calm while patiently
He warmed his hands o'er the embers red,
Then drank with relish the long cold tea
From the sandstone ledge above my bed.

He sat so still, so peaceful there,
I knew he was a friend,
Then high above in the cold night air
I heard the stir of wind.

Soft and sweet, on the wind unfurled,
Came haunting strains of music played
As if all the old masters of the world
Had gathered to serenade.

At first so faint, so soft, so low,
Gently, slowly it louder grew
And somehow I seemed to know
The tale it told was true.

It told the story of a wandering boy,
Of his journeys day by day,
Of the peace, serenity and joy
He encountered on his way.

Vaughn Short

It played a dance for the tumbleweeds
A melody of a cool aspen glade,
Of meadow green where the wild deer feeds
And a rest in the forest's shade.

It sang of canyons stained and red,
Played a rhapsody of twisted trees,
Far vistas with blue sky overhead,
And leaves trembling in the breeze—

Of wafting wind behind a summer shower,
The smell of sage after rain,
How green the ferns in a hidden bower
All in this sweet refrain.

Melodies of far views from a mountain top,
Of sandstone canyons deep and sheer,
Of the towering cliff with awesome drop
And the seasons of the year—

A song of the flitting butterfly,
Of blossoms by the trail,
Floating clouds in an azure sky,
Of beauty where all words fail.

The boy he sat with face serene
As the music cast its spell.
I knew these things he'd lived and seen
As the sweet music rose and fell.

But suddenly the tempo changed,
Quickened the drums—loud they banged.
The symphony was rearranged
Above shrill music cymbals clanged.

So harsh the brass, so loud the strings
As the beat faster and faster grew.
I tried to comprehend these things.
It was a tragedy, this I knew.

Raging River, Lonely Trail

The music told of pain and death,
As I cowered in bed with fear,
But I tried to follow as I held my breath,
And cursed myself for an untrained ear.

But what transpired I do not know,
And I looked at the youth by the fire.
Dazed he sat as though struck a blow
By this symphony so dire.

The music raced on with a savage beat,
Then with a deafening crash it stopped!
Once again notes, soft and sweet,
On the cold night air were dropped.

The boy relaxed—this I could see
His face serene but pale.
Then he turned about and spoke to me,
"I am the spirit of the trail."

"I am the one who's gone before.
In reverence long ago I trod.
Most humbly I did explore
These handiworks of God."

"My spirit wanders by your side
Wherever you do go.
On trail it matches stride for stride
And it basks in your campfire's glow."

"I walk with you in the morning air.
I laze with you at noon.
My presence it is everywhere
From rising sun to waning moon."

"The beauty of this love of mine
I do my best to share—
The desert stark—The stately pine,
The crystal mountain air."

Vaughn Short

"Why come you here perhaps to find,
Some tattered rag, some bit of bone,
Remnants of something long behind,
Reminders of things best left alone?"

"Why seek these out when all around
In every niche, in every vale,
The beauties of the world abound?
These are the true treasures of the trail."

"Every step along the way
New wonders do unfold.
Miracles occur every day,
If you look about and behold."

As the youth talked on, I sleepy grew.
It had been a long hard day.
Suddenly, before I knew,
I'd drifted far away.

At dawn's first glow I looked about
For some little tell-tale clue.
It seemed so real—and yet the doubt,
Was this stranger really true?

No footprints there in the fallen snow,
Yet, deep remains the mystery,
Had I dreamed—or was it really so?
There set my empty cup of tea!

"I shivered as I stoked my fire"

This old world is in sad shape. That, no one can deny, and the picture grows ever gloomier. Aerosol sprays threaten the ozone layer. The air below grows ever murkier as industry and automobiles spew forth their filth. The fish grow unfit to eat as poisons are spread into the sea by the polluted rivers. Not a year passes but a new crisis develops. The day of total disaster draws ever nearer, but that short-sighted unbalancer of nature called "man" lives for the moment. "To hell with future generations! Let them solve their own problems!" That seems to be his attitude. To date, he has shown little inclination to reverse the trend—to make the necessary sacrifices, to slow down that stampede toward the inevitable day of demise. It isn't as if he hasn't been warned. The so called purveyors of "gloom and doom" haven't been silent. I add my meager bit to the unheeded clamor.

THE HOUR IS LATE

By a lonesome fire I sat one night,
Where the giant cactus loomed high.
Shadows flickered as my fire burned bright,
And the crescent moon in the starry sky
Lit the desert with a haunting light,
Then I heard a coyote's lonely cry.

Vaughn Short

I shivered as I stoked my fire,
And it was not from the cold—
But a deep response to a warning dire—
To a spine chilling message truthfully told,
And it said, "Beware for the hour is late,
And you've got this world in a pitiful state.
Man, you must change your ways and soon,
Or else prepare to face your fate.
For as I said before, the hour is late."
This the coyote wailed to the crescent moon.

By a lonesome fire I sat one night
Where aspens stood straight and tall.
Fire reflected off trunks of white
And the moon o'er head was a yellow ball,
That bathed the forest in mellow light,
Then I heard a poor-will's plaintive call.

I shivered as I stoked my fire,
And it was not from the cold—
But a deep response to a warning dire—
To a spine chilling message truthfully told,
And it said, "Beware for the hour is late
And you've got this world in a pitiful state.
Man, you must change your ways and soon,
Or else prepare to face your fate.
For as I said before, the hour is late!"
This the poor-will cried to the yellow moon.

By a lonesome fire I sat one night,
In a clearing among the oak.
The moon was a sliver that gave no light.
And as I listened to the forest folk,
Faint, far away and out of sight,
A phantom owl in the darkness spoke.

I shivered as I stoked my fire,
And it was not from the cold—
But a deep response to a warning dire—
To a spine chilling message truthfully told,

And it said, "Beware for the hour is late
And you have this world in a pitiful state
Man, you must change your ways and soon,
Or else prepare to face your fate.
For as I said before, the hour is late."
Thus the phantom owl spoke to a sliver moon.

So tonight we sit by a cheerful blaze,
And it's good to be out here.
But the coyote spoke of limited days.
The poor-will cried the end is near.
The phantom owl said change your ways,
And they spoke the truth I fear.

So I shiver as I stoke the fire,
And it is not from the cold—
But a deep response to a warning dire—
To a spine chilling message truthfully told,
And it says, "Beware the hour is late,
For you have this world in a pitiful state.
Man, you must change your ways and soon
Or else prepare to meet your fate
For time is fleeting and the problem great."

God help us, phantom moon!

"Out of the south the hawk-faced legions came"

Years back, near the little community of Palominos, where Arizona State Highway Ninety-Two crosses the San Pedro River, there was a sign commemorating Coronado. "Up the broad valley of the San Pedro, forty years before the landing of the pilgrims ...", that's the way it started. I liked that sign. It conjured up lots of dreams—visions of vain Coronado in his armor of gold, followed by his clanking conquistadores.

The San Pedro flows a northward course. Coronado had followed it up out of Mexico. In my youth, the little town of Hereford, a few miles down river from the border, was one of the largest cattle shipping points in the country. Back then, big cattle drives came up out of Mexico following the long ago path of the conquistadores. Where in Mexico these drives originated, or how far they traveled, I don't know, but they were impressive. The rangy, multi-colored, long-horned steers; the whiskered Mexican vaqueros; the saddles with rawhide dally ropes coiled beneath the horn, and always the tapaderos covering the stirrups; the big rowled spurs; the much-branded, trail-weary horses; the taste of powdered dust in the air; the low rumble of driven cattle—these things you don't forget. I loved to see those big herds pass. I consider myself fortunate, for it was the end of an era. Hoof and mouth disease soon closed the border. I'm sure these scenes were not dissimilar to the big drives out of Texas to Abilene.

In those days, I would sometimes sit atop the mountains over-

Raging River, Lonely Trail

looking the San Pedro, and amidst the shimmer of the heat waves below, the shadowy forms of Spanish knights in saddle would pass before my eyes. When I decided to write a few things about Grand Canyon, it was only natural for me to think back to Coronado and the discovery. I had tasted the dust of the trail herds. Coronado's army had powdered this same soil.

GRAND CANYON
The discovery 1540

Out of the south, the hawk-faced legions came
To claim the land in the King's good name,
Searching for seven cities of gold
By the friar, de Niza told.

Up from Mexico, Coronado leads his band
Across the hostile desert land,
Ever northward this great display of might.
The red man trembled at the awesome sight.

Sitting astride his long-eared beast,
Behind the leader rode the priest,
Cloaked in robes and religious zeal,
Converting the savage with Spanish steel.

Next the conquistadores, gaunt and lean,
Sun glinting off the metal's sheen,
Proud and aloof each rider sits,
Silver saddles, silver bits.

Sword clanking on each armored thigh,
Lances at stirrup pointing high,
Lo, the poor natives stood aghast
As Coronado's army past.

A thousand Indians form the rear,
Burdened beneath the armies gear.
Bundles on each banded head,
With weary step they slowly tread.

Vaughn Short

One day a messenger brought the word
A mighty river flowed, he'd heard,
In a great canyon to the north.
The commander summoned his captains forth.

Then he spoke of his intent,
An expedition would be sent.
Captain Cardenas to the north would go;
To check the course of this river's flow.

Across wastelands toward towering peaks,
This canyon vast, Cardenas seeks.
And now the peaks are to the rear.
And still no canyon does appear.

Perhaps this deep down flowing stream
Was just a myth or a foolish dream.
But still the Captain forward pressed,
His weary troops he gave no rest.

Now they tread through forests green,
And still no river can be seen.
But one day they break out through the trees,
And the Captain gasps at the sight he sees!

Before them the whole world seemed to sink,
As they stood there on the canyon brink,
Bold soldiers, stricken, filled with awe,
Wondering if 'twas so, this sight they saw.

Breathtaking stood Grand Canyon then,
Discovered by so called civilized men.
Wondrous will the big gorge stay
Long after man has passed away.

"What happened to those people down below"

In an Ed Abbey book there is a fictional river guide called, "Seldom Seen Smith." If you've read about old Seldom, then you'll know that he wouldn't be about to let the Bureau of Reclamation put one over on him. They might dry up his river but he wouldn't knuckle under easily. He'd be down in the bottom with wheels on his boat, pulling it through the boulders.

In April, May, and into June of 1977, the water was low in Grand Canyon. The Bureau just wasn't letting it through Glen Canyon Dam. They were being very stingy. Most of the boating companies weren't operating. A few rugged, persistent personalities were rowing small boats and meeting their schedules. You'd expect to find old Seldom Seen among this group.

The following is a mostly true, but not completely factual account of a river trip during this low water period. It was a strange trip, the water so clear you could often see bottom. The boats maneuvered between rocks not even seen at higher water. There were rapids where rapids had never been before. I didn't make it all the way through. Because of a tight time schedule, I climbed out, leaving the rest of the party down below.

Rowing the boats were: Kim Crumbo, Mark Crumbo, Stuart Reeter, Bob Shelton, Ken Sleight, and Bob Whitney.

Vaughn Short

SELDOM SEEN AND HIS MACHO CREW

They say the river can't be run.
The water's down—It can't be done.
But if anyone can shoot it through,
It's old Seldom Seen and his macho crew.
So load on the Coors, lash it down!
Might as well be happy if we're going to drown!
Roll up the bow line! Push out the boat!
With all this beer it may not float.

But the boats stay up! We're on our way!
Will we see Houserock by the end of day?
At Badger Rapids the boatmen curse,
The rocks stick up and it couldn't be worse.
So they walk the bank, and they rant and swear.
They shake their heads and they tear their hair.
Then they jump in their boats and bounce on through.
But one hangs up! Now what'll we do?

We push and shove and heave on rope.
The water pours in—there's not much hope.
We pull and tug 'til the boat's unstuck
With a little work, and a lot of luck!
Next we come to old Soap Creek,
The boats they bounce and the oarlocks squeak.
The boys row hard and make the run,
But the sun hangs low, the day most done.

There were Kim and Mark—the Crumbo two,
A couple of Bobs, and a guy called Stu
Making up that macho crew.
And a kid named "Coke" was swamping.

On we push to old Houserock,
Everyone climbs out, and it's quite a shock.
The boatmen say, "We need time to think.
Let's stop here for a night to drink."
Early in the morning to the boatmen's despair
The water's still low and the rapid's still there.

Raging River, Lonely Trail

So they ponder and study and fret and stew,
Then climb in their boats and row right through!

The days they pass, and the going's slow.
The wind is up and the water's low.
We stop at the Little Colorado to take a swim,
Our time's half gone and it's looking grim.
At Carbon Creek we feed the pet raven, Sam,
While we curse the Bureau and we curse the dam.
Swamper throws a mud ball at that old black crow
Stuart says, "Now we're jinxed for down below."

Shove off next morning with mileage to make,
But the Bureau is stingy—won't give us a break.
We're way behind schedule, but little is said
Until someone yells, "There's a rapid ahead!"
Mark goes first, rowing right on track,
Then he turns around and he shouts back,
"To the right of the standing wave, then take it straight!"
But the skipper goes aground, and the problem's great.

There were Kim and Mark—the Crumbo two,
A couple of Bobs, and a guy called Stu
Making up that macho crew.
And a kid named "Coke" was swamping.

The boatmen row back and the going's tough.
The rocks are big and the water's rough.
They all pitch in and they tie on rope.
The boat swings free—once more there's hope.
Six days gone, we're still at Hance.
The people swear, there's not a chance,
But the boatmen do it, possible or not—
Shoot their eight-foot boats through a six-foot slot!

Eight days gone and the girls get prettier.
The beer tastes better and the men are wittier.
But time's running out, and the food is low,
I'm beginning to think it's time to go.
Old Seldom climbs out, and so do I.
Left before sun-up without saying goodbye,
Climbed the walls of that canyon grand,
Left the people sleeping there on the sand.

Vaughn Short

What happened to the people down below?
I can't say and I may never know.
They might have pushed right on through,
In the able hands of that macho crew,
Or might be they stranded way up high,
Top of a rock where the water rushed by,
And sitting there, I greatly fear,
They slowly perished for want of beer.

There were Kim and Mark—The Crumbo two,
A couple of Bobs, and a guy named Stu
Making up that macho team,
That rowed the boats for Seldom Seen.

"The silver bells go jing-a-ling as the little people dance"

Our present world is full of cynics. I've been told there are even folks around who do not believe in the little people—the gremlins, the goblins, the elves, the leprechauns, and all the rest of the magical ones. If you happen to be a nonbeliever, then you have yourself a problem. Struggle along the best you can. It's true these little fellows aren't seen nearly as often as in days of yore. Flighty people they are by nature, so why should they choose to hang around this super-hyperactivated society of ours. If you had a chance, wouldn't you too withdraw to the periphery? I've heard, that when electricity came to Ireland, the leprechauns left. That goes to show what sharp thinking little dudes they are. If you do your thing best in the shadows and the dark, why hang around in the glare of light bulbs?

The tales of by-gone days are full of the little people, but today they are seldom seen. Yet, they must still be frisking about somewhere. Their lifestyle just didn't click with modem ways. Why not move out to less frantic areas?

Have you ever been down in a gloomy canyon and came upon a little hidden bower laced in the greenest of ferns, sparkling with crystal droplets of water? What a perfect home for a fairy princess, you think. Do you recall that sandstone grotto in a twisting water course, the one just right for some grumpy, old elf to do his grumbling? Because they weren't home when you walked by means nothing. For them to disappear at the sound of footsteps is smart and logical.

Suppose the little creature had stayed around to engage you in friendly conversation. What could it learn from a mere mortal that it didn't already know in its vast wisdom? Man is untrustworthy at his best. Why should the little guy risk having a coat tossed over him and being carried out to the very world he is trying to escape? Why risk being toted away to face the glare of T. V. cameras and all the rest of the hullabaloo? Why be humiliated, just so the captor can have his moment of glory in the limelight, and appear on the evening news?

Have I ever seen the little people dance at Elves Chasm? No, I haven't, but then I've never been there when the conditions were right. Have other people? Well, possibly. If so, what would you expect them to do? Return home and run around the block chanting, "I saw an elf, I saw an elf!"? Wouldn't there be those who would look askance at behavior of this type? Some things are better kept to yourself.

ELVES CHASM

At a very special time of the night,
When the moon shines gold and round,
And the river shimmers in the light,
And the water is the only sound.

Down glimmers a little moonbeam
Into the depths of a chasm deep.
On a magic spot it casts its gleam
Where the walls are sheer and steep.

In the mystic light a form appears,
And it stands on a narrow shelf.
Off its tiny face the moonbeam veers
And Lo!—'Tis a wee small elf!

In tinkling droplets, water falls
Into a crystal pool below.
The light rebounds off verdant walls
Where it casts an eerie glow.

Then the elf picks up a silver flute,
And on it plays a lilting tune,
"Oh come you out 'neath rock and root.
Come dance 'neath the big round moon."

Out from a score of secret spots
Where each little creature dwells,
A tiny elf, he forward trots
In pointed boots with silver bells.

In time to the flute each small foot taps,
As they wiggle their round little rears.
They bob their heads 'neath tasseled caps
As they waggle their pointed ears.

They all join hands and form a ring,
And they circle, dip, and prance.
The silver bells go jing-a-ling
As the little people dance.

High above, the flute plays shrill,
And the stars they come and go,
While the dancers dance a gay quadrille
In the moonbeam's eerie glow.

Then suddenly the music quits.
The little moonbeam's no longer there.
Fast, fast away each elf he flits
To the depths of his secret lair.

Perhaps at the chasm when the moon is bright,
If by some lucky, incredible chance,
It's a special time on a magical night—
Then you might see this elfin dance.

"On unhearing ears the words were talked"

On Memorial Day, in 1974, a small dedicated group picketed the Visitors Center at Glen Canyon Dam. The Appellate Court had struck down a previous ruling of the Superior Court that stated that water could not lawfully be allowed to encroach into Rainbow National Monument. The Supreme Court had, by one vote, refused to review the case. The pickets hoped to call public attention to the hazard of the water soon to be under Rainbow Bridge. Without regard for the environment, the level of Lake Powell was being raised to add water to a lake already backing into the Canyonlands country.

I've heard the arguments about the harmless effect of water under Rainbow Bridge. Sure, I know it stands on Kayenta sandstone, a much finer grained formation than the Navajo sandstone of which the bridge is composed. Sure, I know this doesn't absorb water at the rate of the softer Navajo sandstone. Sure, I know the government has sophisticated instruments that can detect the slightest movement of the bridge. I, for one, remain a skeptic. Somewhere down the line, my faith in the reports and statistics of some government bureaus has became somewhat tarnished. Their data seems, so often, to be twisted to become self-serving.

I stood below Rainbow Bridge back in the days when people had more faith in government—back in the days when it was still believed they would honor their commitments and keep their damn lake away. Even then, we talked of what would happen if water ever stood under the big arch.

The Kayenta sandstone lays in flat strata with softer seams between. The eroding of these soft seams is what worries me. From the creek bottom you could climb to the base of the bridge using these strata cracks. It was as easy as climbing a ladder. Despite all propaganda to the contrary, or call it hard facts if you prefer, I firmly believe that Rainbow Bridge will topple in the lifetime of people now living. No, I don't think it will be tomorrow or the day after, but the bridge is doomed. What do I base this on? Why, just standing beneath it and looking around. In no way do I claim to be an expert, but I put in eight years of my life drilling and blasting hard rock. In time you get a feeling about rock, about what is substantial and what is not. In an underground mine it can be the difference between life and death. I put a great deal of faith in feelings. I feel very uneasy about Rainbow Bridge with water penetrating those soft seams.

I left the little group of pickets at noon that Memorial Day, and I was very sad. They were good friends, good people, the best. I didn't want to leave, but necessity dictated it. Just outside of Page, I stopped my pick-up for a young fellow with an ailing motorcycle. He was looking for a ride for himself and bike to Flagstaff. After we were underway, I discovered he was from Tucson, which is also my home. I was able to give him a far longer lift than he had hoped for. As the miles passed, on our long trek down state, we chatted about this and that, but in the back of my mind, the indignities to Rainbow were burning. By the time we reached Tucson, a farewell poem was firmly entrenched in my mind. This poem is for Ken Sleight. He made a long and valiant fight to save Rainbow. He did more than anyone.

Farewell to Rainbow

Sacred Rainbow standing high,
With saddened heart we say goodbye,
To lose you when there was no need,
Victim of a heartless breed,
Victim of the white man's greed.

For centuries majestically you stood.
It seemed as though you always would,
But doomed you were from the very day
When the Piute, Nasha Begay
Led the white man first your way.

Vaughn Short

Long had the Indian known you there,
A sacred shrine, a place of prayer,
Nestled in your canyon deep,
Fast by a revered mountain steep,
Where the Gods of the ancient sleep.

The white man came and he stood in awe,
Deeply moved by the sight he saw.
Around you in the red rock and shifting sand,
He established a monument to this great land
Pledging that you would always stand.

But greed it seems to have its way.
High principals before the dollar sway.
Doomed you were by scheming men
When with casual stroke of pen,
They authorized a dam in Glen.

"No water in the monument," they did swear!
"Never a drop to enter there!"
Staunch they made this solemn pledge,
Never to waiver—Never to hedge,
But the greedy drove their dividing wedge.

"How foolish all this needless fear.
What harm a little water here?
Those who protest know not the fact."
So said the schemers with guileful tact,
To cover up their shameful act.

Those who could save you turned away.
At last there came the fateful day.
To hear your plight, the courts they balked.
On unhearing ears the words were talked.
All in vain the pickets walked.

Raging River, Lonely Trail

And so we watch with great chagrin
As water rises up from Glen.
At your very foundations it does lap.
Ever eroding, your strength to sap.
All so unnecessary this great mishap.

So, sacred Rainbow, standing high,
With saddened heart we say goodbye.
Sad the condolences that we send.
(It's always hard to lose a friend.)
We love you to the very end.

But when no longer high you stand
Above this great red sandstone land,
Those who knew you way back when,
Back before the rape of Glen,
Pledge to fight on. Fight on to win!

"Columbus was only the first tourist"

From three directions we were approaching rendezvous point, converging in on that old log corral that butts up against the sandstone where Kane Creek cuts the Cedar Mesa. I had driven up from Southern Arizona, dropped down from the pine forests at Flagstaff, and entered the far distances of Navajo country. In Indian land I had spent the night. Through early morning light I drove past the backdrop of Monument Valley, then steeply descended into the little river town of Mexican Hat, Utah. From there my pick-up truck labored up the steep, winding Moki Dugway and topped out onto Cedar Mesa. Meeting point was now only twenty miles away and I was first to arrive.

A group from the Wilderness Society, with outfitter, Ken Sleight, was on its way from Green River, taking the Lake Powell-Fry Canyon route. The pack stock was being provided by Pete Steele: cowboy, guide, basketweaver, and superb campfire storyteller. With mules in truck, he would be rolling in from Monticello, down over the Comb Ridge. We were all going to take a trip through the Grand Gulch.

I strolled about, getting the kinks out, waiting. I seated myself at the back of the corral, leaned up against the friendly sandstone that rose in a thirty-foot wall, and soaked in the welcome warmth of the sun. It was April. At the start of numerous trips we had penned our mules here. I had made camp at this very spot more than once, waiting for a group to join me the next day. There were lots of memories. Once, I had slept the night beneath the protecting overhang of the wall while the rain came down without mercy.

I took out my pencil and note pad. I always start trips with the best intentions of keeping a journal. I wrote down the account of my trip up through the Indian country. The following poem was later garnered from these pages. It was not consciously intended to be poetry at the time of writing.

We had a great trip through Grand Gulch.

THOSE OLD ONES

Where do they come from, those old ones
Who stand on the edge of nowhere
Out in vast Navajo land,
With pink buttes hazy in the distance
And the air filled with fine sand, blowing?

I stopped on the edge of the asphalt ribbon,
The white man's intrusion.
I waited for the old one to slide onto the seat beside me.
The smell of cheap wine invaded.

The exchange of names, his muttered low
But a name with dignity.
With such names fierce warriors once rode forth,
Heads held high.

The handshake limp,
A white man's custom but not of his ways.
And he labored under the burden of conversation
He felt was expected.

"This land is dry, much too dry, not worth much."
And he gestured vaguely out beyond,
Out toward the pink buttes, hazy through sand filled air.

Then he spoke of Columbus.
'He was not the first," he said.
"Not like they teach in schools.
The Navajo and Hopi were already here."

"How true," I agreed.
"Columbus was only the first tourist."
Pleased he repeated it, fixing it in his mind,
"Columbus was only the first tourist."

Out in vast Navajo land,
Out on the edge of nowhere,
With the pink buttes hazy in the distance
And the air filled with fine sand, blowing,
I let him off, that old one.

Where do they go?
I drove on down the asphalt ribbon,
The white man's intrusion,
And I opened the windows to clear the smell of
    cheap wine.

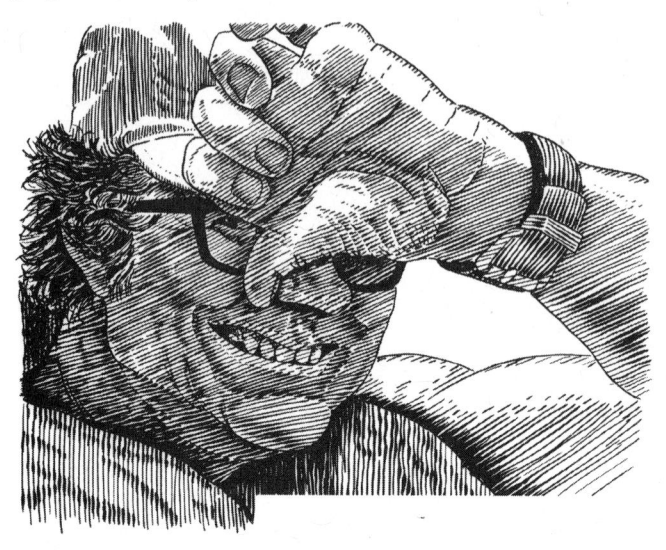

"I may not be like your other children"

Most people seem to enjoy poetry read aloud in outdoor settings. The wilder and more remote the area, the bigger hit it seems to make.

Over the years, I've read a lot around campfires, sometimes holding a flashlight for illumination. Often I've recited from memory. One poem that's always been a favorite, and understandably so, is Badger Clark's "The Cowboy's Prayer." On a pack trip with horses and mules about, it seemed appropriate. On the white water river trips, I always felt the boatmen deserved a prayer of their own. With this in mind I wrote one for them. Like the cowboy, the river people cover a wide spectrum of individuals. There are many on the river, however, who can identify with this poem.

A Boatman's Prayer

Dear Lord, here on this river bank
Before we launch today,
Please, listen for a moment
To what a boatman has to say.

Now I don't claim to be a saint,
And my soul's not lily white.
Sometimes I yield to temptation.
Sometimes I drink too much at night.

Down here I'm not an angel,
Don't even want to talk about the town
With all its woes and pitfalls
And the things that get you down.

So I'm really in no position
To ask for much from you,
But if You could see the way,
Please, try and hear me through.

Life down here's a pleasure
And there's beauty everywhere.
So I'm really not complaining
In my humble little prayer.

The thing I'm trying to get across,
In my stumblin', bumblin' way,
Is a boatman, he's not really bad,
No matter what they say.

But a boatman's life's not easy,
Although I'm not trying to alibi.
There's no turning back up the river,
It's no use to even try.

Whatever lies before you
You've got to see it through.
You can't stop halfway
And back off and start anew.

It's just things aren't as easy
As they look to those outside.
It's more than jumping in a boat
And going for a ride.

Now, I'm not too worried
About what's down the way,
'Cause I've done this many times before
When I didn't even pray.

Raging River, Lonely Trail

Oh! I don't take it lightly!
I've always got to know,
There's an old lion a roarin'
In the river down below.

But we'll make it through the rapids
There'll be no problem there.
That's not the reason
For me to say this prayer.

The reason I'm a talkin',
And it's not easy for me to say,
Just, please, don't view us boatmen
In the ordinary way.

I love this world You made us,
And I love the rivers too.
I like the things that are simple,
And I like the work I do.

But could You sort of look the other way
And a few small things forgive?
For it's a little different,
This kind of life I live.

I have no neighbors watching
To see what I do each day,
So it's just a little easier
To stray off the narrow way.

Now I have no church to go to.
They just aren't built down here.
But I see Your walls and canyons,
And I feel You very near.

Now, I'm standing here a rattlin',
I've talked for quite a spell.
I still can't seem to get across
What I'm trying to tell.

It's, "Just please try to overlook
Some of the things I do.
I may not be like your other children,
But I feel very close to You."

                                            Amen

"...and Maggie smiled at me"

It's a big, wonderful world out there! Of course I'm speaking about that part of it that still has some semblance of wilderness. But no matter how awesome, the country you traverse, it's the people with you who make the trip. If they really get caught up in the beauty of the experience, and most do, it's going to be a great outing.

People may come from far corners, represent many professions, and span generations. Throw them together on a back pack or a boating trip, and in short time they unite into a family. I consider myself very fortunate for the opportunities I have had to meet so many fine people out where the life is simple—out where folks are at their very best.

We were boating the Grand Canyon. It was early in the season. The group was small and congenial; a good bunch. it was a first rate trip all the way. At Dubendorff Rapid, I went ashore to photograph the triple-rig shooting the white water. Back at the boat (just making conversation) I said to one of the girls, "Maggie, you didn't smile for the photographer." She promised a big smile the next time. Next time happened to be Lava Falls—that old granddaddy of a rapid. You who are familiar with Lava know it isn't a smiling situation. Maybe Stuart, "The Mountain Man," and a few other boatmen can laugh all the way through, but that isn't for everyone.

A triple-rig always gives a thrilling ride through Lava Falls. I snapped some good pictures. When I rejoined the group Maggie said, "I was smiling for you. I was watching for you when we went over the top and I was smiling!" It isn't everyday a girl smiles at you from the midst of a million tons of frothing water. I appreciated the effort. I remembered. At home I received a rather sad, little letter from Maggie.

It had been a memorable adventure. She hadn't wanted to leave the river. Out of Vegas, the plane hit turbulence, and she thought of the rapids and cried all the way to Los Angeles. She wanted me to know that she had enjoyed the poetry around the campfires at night. It had added to the experience. It had been a super trip for me also, so when I answered Maggie's letter I made a sincere effort to return the compliment. I sent a little verse, that to the best of my memory, went something like this:

THE LITTLE THINGS

As I look back o'er times that are past,
And fond memories I recall,
It's the little fleeting things that last.
Important things are usually small.

Dreaming back through many years
Of both happiness and despair
The taste of salty tears—
A caress on silken hair.

Laughter on a moonlit walk
Over some silly little rhyme—
Time when there was no need to talk
A hand tucked snug in mine—

A twinkle in mischievous eye
Above a wrinkled nose
Memory of a tender sigh
Sweet breast that fell and rose—

So the things that I recall,
The sweetness and the pain,
To some would matter not at all.
They think of worldly gain.

Should someone ask, "What have you done?
What accomplishments are there to see?"
Why, I saw a boat a rapid run,
And Maggie smiled at me.

Raging River, Lonely Trail

"The shadows are deep and the light is dim where the wild water froths and flows"

Belle Zabor is a big rapid—a very big rapid—the kind that chews you up and then forgets to spit you out. What's its rating? That's generally the first question asked about a rapid. Well, I've heard considerable discussion on this, and of course there is always some disagreement. However, it is generally agreed that on the one to ten scale, it's somewhere between an eleven and a fourteen—depending, as all rapids do, on the water at a given time.

On runs through Grand Canyon, if we have a good group, which most are, then we save the ballad about Belle until the night after Lava Falls. At that time it goes over big. If we have a not so good bunch then we recite the ballad sitting at the top of Lava waiting to go through. This presents a problem though, as then the boatmen decide they are going to walk it. Rumor and evidence to the contrary, boatmen aren't so stupid!

Nostalgia brought about "The Ballad of Belle Zabor." No one likes to see the end of a river trip. For me the withdrawal pains are acute, followed by slow months of longing. The deep canyons, the thrill of the rapids—you don't shake them. The pull of the canyon country is always there. I do a lot of drifting and dreaming in those long periods between trips. Most of the time my mind is pretty well detached. I can get plenty of confirmation on that. "Belle Zabor" is the product of waiting for a river season to start. I had it pretty well thought out before I picked up a pencil. Still the poem turned out different then I had visualized. This is often the way of long ballads. They seem to have a will of their own. I had about half the verses flitting around in the dark crannies of my mind. I put them on paper and began filling in, writing connecting verses. Building bridges I call this to myself. In my circle, you don't talk about building bridges out loud. Although this is a lengthy ballad, once I picked up the pencil, it went very fast.

Why the name "Belle Zabor?" Because it has a nice poetic ring to my ear and it's a snap to rhyme with. I had no particular rapid, place, or person in my mind. It is dreamed up in its entirety.

The first time I recited it around a campfire was on a cold, October trip in the Canyon of Ladore. Afterwards someone asked a boatman if he would like to run the Belle. He was very emphatic. He didn't even want to know where that S.O.B. was!

This poem is for all those great guys and gals who row for Ken Sleight Expeditions, and for Moki Mac.

THE BALLAD OF BELLE ZABOR

From a canyon deep, from a canyon dark,
From a canyon steeped in gloom,
The listening ear can always hear
A deep pitched song of doom.

Far beneath the rim of this canyon grim
Speeds a river wrought with woes.
And the shadows are deep, and the light is dim
Where the wild water froths and flows.

The walls are sheer in this canyon drear.
In the river huge boulders lie,
And they cause the water to surge and boil,
And they cause the spray to fly.

At one wild turn where the waters churn
The bottom drops away,
There the river falls on the rocks below
And the air is filled with spray.

Raging River, Lonely Trail

In a frightening whirl the waters swirl
And they form a deep dark hole.
Around its edges the rocks are ringed.
To make the huge waves roll.

For miles around can be heard the sound
Of this rapid's mighty roar.
And a tale is told of how it got its name
The name of Belle Zabor.

Smooth as a dream this raging stream
At the mouth of the canyon flows,
And there on its banks in yesteryears
A tiny hamlet rose.

In a grassy vale at the end of a trail
That wound from the winding street,
A woodsman dwelt in a cabin of log,
Kept by his daughter sweet.

With a temper quick, not one to trick,
The woodsman guarded the maiden well.
Old Zeke Zabor was not one to cross
And he worshipped his daughter Belle.

Now they tell of this daughter Belle,
Of her beauty and her charm,
And how old Zeke watched night and day
To keep this maid from harm.

But there came one day a riverman
With charm and wit to spare,
And he lulled old Zeke with good red wine
While he wooed the maiden fair.

Soft as a breeze in the whispering trees
He murmured vows of the eternal kind,
And not at all did the maid suspect
The fickleness of a riverman's mind.

Vaughn Short

Fast in her arms he reveled in her charms
While in a stupor old Zeke lay.
When the poor girl slept then her lover crept,
To the river he stole away.

He climbed in his boat and put it afloat,
Pulled hard for the middle of the stream.
The moon came out and the stars were bright
And the whole world seemed a dream.

All seemed so right in that balmy night
'Til he felt the currents tow.
He leaned to his oars and he gave it his best,
But his boat swept on down below.

He knew he was doomed when the canyon loomed,
But he made a hell of a fight.
The water raged as the walls grew high
And shut out the last of the light.

No time to repent for a life misspent
Or regrets for things left undone.
No time to recall the bad and the good
Or the things done in the name of fun.

He gave no cry when his boat leaped high
And his oars pulled only air.
Then he was down in the swirling hole
No time for a muttered prayer.

Though his heart was stout, time ran out,
From the shattered boat he was thrown.
The dark waters surged up over his head
And the river claimed him for its own.

The very next day they found where he lay
In an eddy by the rock strewn shore.
They lifted him out and carried him away
To the grief stricken Belle Zabor.

Raging River, Lonely Trail

At a total loss by a new formed cross,
Belle wept in wild dismay,
As she flung herself on the new raised mound
Where her ill-fated lover lay.

With a wailing sound she leaped from the ground
To the raging river she fled!
For her life had no meaning left
With her lover cold and dead.

Where the wild waters swept with a scream she leapt
And the rapid took her forever more.
When it took her life it took her name,
For now they call it Belle Zabor.

Now they say at night when the stars are bright
And the moonbeams flit around,
From out of the din of the rapid's roar
Can be heard a sweet, sweet sound.

'Tis music played by the long dead maid
As she pleads with the men on the shore,
"Oh cast your craft on my plunging waves.
Come run the Belle Zabor.

In the little vale at the end of the trail
Old Zeke lived out his remaining days,
Then the cabin was empty, the windows dark,
The old place was falling to stays.

But one bright day there passed that way
A young man with his son and his wife,
And he saw the old cabin and at once he knew
'Twas a dream he'd dreamed all his life.

From dawn to night 'til the cabin was right
He toiled with his wife and the lad.
And there they dwelt and all was well.
It was a good, good life they had.

But one night late came the hand of fate
And the song of Belle he heard.
He did not know what troubled his mind
For he recognized not a word.

As the days progressed like a man possessed
He brooded and he knew not why.
Deeper and deeper his mind was drawn
To the dead maiden's plaintive cry.

"Oh come and rest on my trembling breast.
Know the sweetest love ever gave.
I'll tell you this, you've never known bliss
Like a visit to my watery grave."

The man never knew as his troubles grew,
'Twas the siren song in his ear
That tugged at his heart and poisoned his mind
And filled his soul with fear.

He could not eat, the song's hypnotic beat
Ever enticed like a deadly lure.
Though he tried and he tried to shut his mind,
'Twas more than he could endure.

The sleep he lost as he turned and tossed
Made his cheeks grow wan and pale.
His temper was short and his moods were dark
And his body grew lean and frail.

In sleep one night came a revealing light.
He leaped from his bed and he swore,
"I am the man! I have the plan!
I'll run the Belle Zabor!"

"I'll build a boat that will ever float,
For I dreamed this in my dream.
It must be strong and it must be stout
And it must be tight of seam."

Raging River, Lonely Trail

"It must take the knock of the jagged rock
And still bounce back for more.
It will be a boat that can not sink,
The likes never built before."

Like a man entranced the risk he chanced
Never entered into his mind.
He vowed he would build his boat
Of the strongest wood he could find.

In the country about he searched throughout
And he selected his material well.
Day after day in a skillful way
His hammer rose and fell.

Stroke by stroke from seasoned oak
He carved his planks to fit.
He sealed them tight with pitch of pine
And the boat grew bit by bit.

Fore and aft as he fashioned the craft,
He built chambers water tight.
He made it wide and broad of beam
So it could tilt and bounce upright.

At last one day before him lay
The boat of his fondest dreams.
And it seemed a very able craft
To run the wildest streams.

His wife implored, but he ignored
Her pleas of not to go
For he said, "It's destined I try my boat
On the rapids down below."

"For I had this dream, and it would seem
The first I was meant to be
To run Belle Zabor with boat and oar.
That is my destiny!"

Despite his wife's fears and her flowing tears,
He launched out in the stream.
He settled himself unto his oars
To fulfill his fleeting dream.

At the waterfall 'neath the towering wall
The rapid roared its siren song—
"Hurry down to me, wild and free,
Your journey won't be long."

With skill and poise, as the approaching noise
Louder and wilder grew,
He tested his craft with the bite of his oars
And the boat responded true.

The moments passed and the time ran fast
'Til before him the rapid lay.
He could not see what waited beyond
In the churning froth and spray.

He went over the top of that awesome drop!
He plunged into the deafening sound!
The water took hold of his thrashing boat
And spun it hard around!

Though sturdy the boat with a strong will to float,
And brave the man at the oar,
They were no match for the fury and wrath
Of the wild rapid, Belle Zabor.

With all his might, he pulled fast to the right,
He tried to avoid the hole.
Hard he crashed into a rock on the rim,
And it caused his boat to roll.

His chances were dim as he tried to swim,
But his efforts were to no avail.
The mad waters dashed him on the rocks
And they broke his body frail.

Raging River, Lonely Trail

The day was sad for the widow and lad.
The walk from the graveyard long.
The mother patted the boy on the head
And bade him be brave and strong.

But when he got his chance the boy in a trance
Into the deep, dark canyon fled.
'Til he stood on the brink of the awesome fall
Filled with fear and dread.

But as the moments flew his passion grew
Until he shook his fist and swore
In a towering rage, "When I come of age
I'll run you, Belle Zabor!"

The years flew fast until at last
The boy left his mother's side.
And her pleading tears were to no avail
To this headstrong youth with pride.

Fast in his head were the words that he said
When he made that childhood vow.
Ever and ever it burned in his mind
And he swore he'd do it now.

His mind was on fire with a wild desire
This rapid he must run!
He set forth into the world
To seek how it could be done.

This fledging boy, he sought not joy.
He had a desperate need
To be able to guide a heaving boat
And a raging rapid read.

At camp on the bars at night 'neath the stars
He heard tales the rivermen told.
And he listened well and he listened long
To the wisdom of the old.

Never before had youth at oar
Strived so hard to learn.
He seldom spoke and he never smiled.
And his manner was cold and stern.

When he did hear be it far or near
Of a river hard to run,
Then he set forth be it south or north
And he ran it not for fun.

He did it to learn, for he did yearn
All the things to know
About the rapids, wild and free,
And how a boatman should row.

How to survive the knock of the jagged rock,
How to avoid the swirling hole,
How to brave the wildest wave,
And what to do in a roll.

As time flew his skill it grew
As a boatman shrewd and strong.
On every stream he was supreme.
He stood above the throng.

As oarsman staunch, wherever boats launch,
They sought his services out,
In times of distress with great finesse
He proved both skilled and stout.

But they thought it sad, this handsome lad
Never smiled or tried to joke.
The rumor grew of an ill-fated love
And how his heart was broke.

For many said at night in bed
On some lonely river shore,
They often heard him toss and turn
And murmur, "Belle Zabor."

Raging River, Lonely Trail

But he was never swayed by winsome maid.
For him life held no fun,
Until he could fulfill his burning need.
This rapid he must run!

Time slipped past and at last
He'd made himself such a name.
At oar of boat he had no peer,
To him all rivers were tame.

Then he knew what he must do.
The time had come and now
He must return to his boyhood home
And fulfill his awesome vow.

The mother was glad to see the lad
But her heart cried out in pain,
"Oh stay away from the river, Son!"
But her pleading was in vain.

He brought with him for his journey grim
The latest boat on the scene.
It was strong and its sides were tough.
It was made of neoprene.

His smile was brave, as a kiss he gave
To his mother on the shore.
Said, "The time is now to fulfill my vow
To the rapid, Belle Zabor."

The water was fast, for in days past
Rains had raised the river's flow.
Never before in such violent rage
Had the rapid roared down below.

His heart beat stout. He had no doubt
As the rapid closer and closer grew.
He'd be the one! He'd be the first
To shoot a boat on through!

He pulled hard to the rear as the rapid grew near
To slow the boat's wild flight,
Then his craft went over the edge
And he dropped down out of sight!

Never before had man at oar
Rowed with such skill and might.
Where the wild waves roll he avoided the hole.
It looked like he'd won his fight!

But at the very last when he tried to slip past
A jagged rock that stuck
Barely above the foaming froth,
The side of his boat he struck.

With a sickening tear he lost the air
In a front compartment of his boat.
Water poured in! He was out of control,
Although he was still afloat!

He could not guide with that deflated side.
His boat flipped in the very next wave
Between rocks on the right his body wedged tight,
And he went to his watery grave.

Raging River, Lonely Trail

If you want to live, this message I give
To all brave rivermen;
Whether you tread the narrow and straight,
Or revel in the deep dark sin.

No matter how bold, if you want to grow old,
Heed what has gone before.
Fulfill your dreams on the wildest streams,
But don't try the Belle Zabor!

Vaughn Short

"It's your own damn fault if you have no fun"

When I set a poem on paper it's usually been bouncing around in my head for a time. Sometimes, I have a few verses that I write down and then I fill in. Once in awhile I have it complete before I ever pick up a pencil. If I have to mull it about in my mind, then it usually sticks with me. If it is too spontaneous, if it comes too fast and easy, then chances are I lose it forever.

This poem is a real puzzler. I don't recall giving it one thought before I wrote it down. Afterwards I was baffled. I still am. Not that the philosophy is foreign because I sometimes think that way, but I can't put my finger on the catalytic agent that turned me on. The mood and the place were all wrong for composing. I was seated at my desk at work, fighting an aspirin-eating headache (one of those that devours the mind and leaves you a listless, non-thinking robot). I picked up a felt tip pen and scribbled the verses down very rapidly on a yellow scratch pad.

Afterwards, even in my dull-witted state, I was somewhat amazed. "Why?", I asked myself, "Why, here of all places?" My rather technical job usually keeps the creative spirit well in check. Why, with my head throbbing? I usually have to be in a light hearted mood or else very emotional to compose poetry.

I looked around at the charts, dials, and pushbuttons of my confining, automated, computerized world and came up with no answer. At that precise moment I was feeling no burning animosity toward the system, no little spirits of rebellion were fanning the flames, the urge to break free was lying dormant. Then why?

I stuffed the yellow scratch paper in my lunch bucket and carried it home. I made very few changes in the original.

Perhaps since my head was rather vacant at the time, my mind may have been out hobnobbing with one of the truly free spirits—one of those rare few who say, "Really what the hell!", then leaves tedium behind and sallies forth into the world to do their thing. The things the rest of us gutless people only dream about.

I read the poem to Joanna Coleman the night before she left to climb in Nepal. She nodded her head in complete agreement all the way through.

Wherever on the mountain you may be, Joanna—Free Spirit—be it mighty Everest, majestic McKinley or little Babo, this one is for you.

Really, What the Hell?

Some live this life at a frenzied pace
As they pursue the almighty dollar,
And the object is to be at the head of the race
Whether they labor or wear a white-collar.
They're all the same
Whether they labor or wear a white-collar.

So let the old World madly spin
As they pursue the almighty dollar,
I'll sit me down on a lonely peak,
Disdainful of the wealth they seek,
And think of the good things as I grin!
I sure will,
I'll think of the good things as I grin!
So spin on, old World, spin!

Some must drive the plush automobiles,
And they mortgage their souls to the banks.
They seem to think it's the cost of their wheels
That sets them above the ranks.
It sure does,
It sets them above the ranks!

So speed old World in headlong flight,
As they mortgage their souls to the banks.
I'll take a stroll this lovely day
And drink in the beauty along the way,
And I'll not toss in my bed tonight.
I won't

I'll not toss in my bed tonight.
Speed on, old World, in headlong flight!

Some always want the best in life,
And they labor long to gain it.
Their days are full of stress and strife,
And they'll break their backs to obtain it.
As sure as hell,
They'll break their back to obtain it.

So let the old World madly whirl,
As they labor long to gain it.
I'll just lie back beneath the trees
And smell sweet flowers in the cooling breeze,
And I'll dream of a beautiful girl
That's me,
I'll dream of a beautiful girl.
So whirl, old World, whirl!

Some look down at the kid by the road,
Thumb held out and clothes that are worn,
They wonder why he don't live by the code,
And they turn up their noses in scorn,
They do,
They turn up their noses in scorn.

So zoom, old World, on your doomsday flight
As they turn up their noses in scorn.
We're all aboard and taking a ride.
There's no way to get off! No place to hide!
Who's to say if he's wrong or right?
How about it?
Who's to say if he's wrong or right?
Zoom on, old World, on your doomsday flight.

Some folks like to make the rules.
But really, what the hell?
Who are the sane and who are the fools?
Only time will tell!
That's right, so right,
Only time will tell.

So plunge on, old World, to the very end.
Really, what the hell?
It's your own damn fault if you have no fun
Before life's little stint is done,
For you're only here for a brief time, friend,
That's straight facts, that is,
You're only here for a brief time, friend,
Plunge on, old World, to the very end.

"I gazed in the campfire's glow"

On the endangered species list is the campfire. I haven't heard any loud drum beating to save it, although its demise is inevitable. I, for one, shall mourn its passing. It's good I came along when I did, campfires have been an important part of my life. More and more they are regulated against. Fewer and fewer are the areas where they are permitted. Below the big dams the driftwood is running out.

My first experience with fire was just one coal's worth. Now one coal of fire may not seem much to you, and it's true it's not a heck of a lot of campfire, but to me at a very early age, its care and tending were an awesome responsibility. My mother would take a glowing coal from the kitchen stove and place it on a bare spot on the ground to make my very own "campfire." No way was I to move it! Fire was grown-up business. To be allowed to step over that invisible barrier and sample the adult world was a privilege not to be taken lightly. If I didn't show the proper respect for fire, there might never be another chance. It was a big burden for young shoulders. Although I liked sitting by my "campfire," I liked the putting out part best. How I loved to hear the coal sizzle. There was water to be carried from the windmill, then my "fire" had to be thoroughly quenched again and again. Those were the rules laid down.

I love campfires. Like to build them, sit by them, smell them, hear them, everything. Gazing into dying embers, I often think of those first ones, those one coal ones. In their time, and in their way, they were as impressive as any. Maybe more so.

Raging River, Lonely Trail

Another early experience with fire was the summer the mountains burned. Never before had there been such a blaze in the Chiricahuas (Cheer-i-cow-was). For days, a smoky pall hung over the countryside. At night, the top of the mountains wore a flaming crown. My Dad was gone most of the summer, up there directing a fire crew. Mother had all the chores. We kids were to small to do much. Each night after milking we would stand in the yard and watch the fire. There was an uneasiness over the whole community. Even a small child could feel it. My mother always talked reassuringly, but it was a scary time. That fire burned itself ever into my mind. The campfires I remember best are the lonely ones.

The following poem came from such a fire-lonely remote, alone.

My Soul

I gazed one night in the campfire's coals
And I saw my soul laid bare,
And it didn't seem like other souls
As I watched it lying there.

Now who would want this well worn soul
With its tarnish and its taint?
'Twas plain to see time had taken its toll,
And it wasn't the soul of a saint.

And yet for all its battered look,
And the year mark when 'twas made,
And the scars from the beating it had took
It wasn't a soul I'd trade.

If I had a soul as pure as snow,
What could I really do?
I'd have to sit and coddle it so,
The pleasures would be few.

If I had a soul tough as a boot,
A soul hard as tempered steel,
Little things wouldn't matter a hoot,
What could I really feel?

Every worn and tender spot
That lets the teardrops flow,
I'd rather have them than not
Than be like some I know.

And those places that are rough,
They help me play my game.
You see I'm really not so tough
Though I try to wear the name.

Though my old soul might need repair,
And some polish it sure could stand,
Some would say it was awfully square
And not worth much second hand—

But as I gazed in the campfire's glow,
I loved it with all my heart.
I wouldn't swap it for any I know,
We couldn't stand to be apart.

"On the side of the hill in old Jerome"

In the old town of Jerome, Arizona, lives Katie Lee. She is a folk singer of note, poet, authoress, and above all a friendly, gracious lady. Katie was on the rivers back before the crowds. She saw the start of the "Baloney Boats" and was not impressed.

Floating with Frank Wright (who took over the Nevills' boats), Katie sang and composed down through the canyons of the Colorado.

Her folk records of the rivers are a must if you are a white water enthusiast. No one is a stauncher foe of Glen Canyon Dam than Katie. She steadfastly refuses to go back through Grand Canyon as long as the dam sets up above. On my way up state for a rowing trip through the Grand, I stopped by Jerome to visit with her. Later, down in the canyon, I wrote these lines for Katie.

For Katie

> Moon peeking over canyon rim
> Changing walls from dark to dim,
> Softly lighting depths below
> Where whispering little breezes blow.
>
> Then the ghost of a river unjustly tamed
> Once so fierce but long since shamed
> Its roaring voice now a plaintive plea Asks,
> "Where, oh where, is Katie Lee?"

On the side of the hill in old Jerome
Pretty Katie sits at home,
Singing of a river free
Rushing down to the merry sea.
Katie can't come back, you know,
Back to the river she misses so.
Can't come back to the rapids roar,
Not 'til the dams are no more.

River dropping out of sight,
Water dashing wild and white,
Waves among the boulders play,
Making rooster tails of frothing spray.
Rocks ringed about the swirling hole
Where huge breakers leap and roll,
From the midst of this roaring din
Asks a voice, "Where's Katie been?"

On the side of the hill in old Jerome
Pretty Katie sits at home,
Dreaming back of long ago
When wild did the Colorado flow.
Katie can't come back, you see,
Not until the river's free.
Can't come back to her one true love
As long as the dam sets up above.

At night within the canyon deep
Listening awhile, awaiting sleep,
Then soft and sweet the river sings
Of sandy beach, of crystal springs,
Pool beneath the waterfall,
Of narrow gorge, of towering wall,
Of water wild where the rapids roar,
Of a singing girl who comes no more.

On the side of the hill in old Jerome
Pretty Katie sits at home,
Thinking back of sadiron boat,
Water free on which to float,

Raging River, Lonely Trail

Oarsman young, strong, and brave
Undaunted by rock or dashing wave.
Oh! Would someone set the Colorado free?
The river needs you, Katie Lee!

Vaughn Short

"There's sandstone canyons in my dreams"

There has been much said and written about the old Glen Canyon. It is gone. Gone forever unless you believe it will be resurrected one of these days. Many do.

I floated Glen three times. Like most trips, you remember the first one best. I had been in the Escalante Canyons for a couple of weeks. I didn't have a lot of time left, but enough to squeeze in one of Ken Sleight's Glen trips. I'd have to make fast tracks for home at the end. That's why I drove down to Arizona, and then with a companion flew back up into Utah for the start. We landed on the old airstrip on the Hite side of the river. At that time almost everyone was using the better strip on the White Canyon side. The plane flew away, and we walked down to the little town which we found deserted.

The road out to Hanksville was washed out by recent storms. This was unknown to us. Across the river, the road to Mexican Hat and Blanding was also gone. Woody, the ferry man, was living over at White Canyon. With the roads out, as they had been for some days, he wasn't paying any attention to the ferry or the little beer-bar he ran at Hite. Two foodless days we spent there. I had lots of time to meditate about Glen Canyon before I ever traversed it. Nights, I spread my sleeping bag under the bar. Don't know how many people have sacked out under the bar at Hite, but it wouldn't be too many. It was well off the beaten path. In the meantime, Ken was busy building road and trying to get down to the river. He never did get his truck to Hite, but he made it down North Wash and launched his boats above us. From there, the party floated down and picked us up. I remember having a very good appetite that first meal. In those days before pavement invaded the red country it was easier to have little

Raging River, Lonely Trail

adventures. It was an enjoyable trip, that first one. And, the second. And, the third. It was a remarkable canyon. The impressions were lasting. If the canyon had survived, I would have returned again and again. Like many others I still mourn its passing. Damn that dam!

A Song of Glen

Tranquil did the river flow
Where once I used to drift and dream
Down a high-walled canyon stream.
That's the Glen I used to know
Before they dammed it down below.

Each day was a new delight
Floating on the water calm,
Drinking in the healing balm,
Thankful for this brief respite
From the world's mad headlong flight.

Drifting under heavens blue
Where high in the red walls above
Trilled the canyon wren of love.
Simple were your needs, and few,
A chance to mend and start anew.

Should you feel the urge to stray
Into side canyons deep and cool
That harbored many a pleasant pool,
There you could splash and play
And while away a perfect day.

But now no longer does it please.
Somewhere fled the quiet and peace,
Somehow the tranquility did cease.
Gone the grasses, gone the trees,
No river riffling in the breeze.

Vaughn Short

Raging River, Lonely Trail

But fond memories will never die,
For now at night it always seems
There're sandstone canyons in my dreams,
Placid river floating by
Reflecting red walls and blue sky.

There're many places I have been,
Many more that I will see,
But nothing like this river free.
How glad I am that way back then
I took the time and floated Glen.

"So many things that you could tell"

"A Kelly in every canyon," that's what they used to say about the Huachuca (waa-choo-ca) Mountains. It wasn't too far from the truth. The Kellys came to the mountains back when Tombstone was in its heyday. The father had been a sheriff of some Texas county before he migrated west with his wife and their large brood—a family that was top heavy with boys. For a time, he worked around the mines in Tombstone and then moved across the San Pedro Valley, settling on the east slope of the Huachuca Mountains at a spot to become known as Kelly's Oak. There he labored with his axe to feed his growing family. Those were the years the big trees were stripped off the mountains. South, in nearby Mexico, the booming mining industry was pleading for timbers to shore up the underground workings. Under the tangle of brush that now covers most of the slopes, you can still see those big rotting stumps of yesteryears' trees.

Before they reached their teens, the Kelly boys were working, walking by the plodding oxen that pulled the heavy, timber-loaded wagons south into Mexico. In time, they became husky enough to work in the mines, and they scattered over Cochise County and Northern Sonora.

Lon Kelly was the one that I knew best. Sometimes he visited our cabin. He would sit by the fire and talk with my Dad for hours. He was an embittered, lonely, old man, but when he forgot the injustice of his present lot, and reminisced of better days, he could make you tingle with excitement. He always complimented my Dad on his cooking. I suspect his menu had been meager and unvaried for many years.

Political unrest had driven him from Mexico. Leaving behind his native wife and their children, he was forced to flee from the revolution. Hiding by day, traveling only in the dark of night, he crept back across the border to his old home mountains, the Huachucas. Most of his brothers' life stories didn't differ too much from his. One-by-one they returned to their beloved mountains—their boyhood home.

When I first came to the Huachucas, the Kellys were in their twilight. Will Kelly had died a couple of years previously. Sick and alone, he had frozen to death in his little cabin high on the north slope of a towering peak. He was buried there in his own prospect hole. Three Kellys remained, each living apart in a remote area. Only Jim had a wife. The depression years had not been easy on the brothers. The bottom had dropped out of the metal market. Still they had eked out an existence with their gold pans. The gravel banks in the Huachucas are stingy, the yellow color seldom in evidence. At times, they broke the hard quartz rock to pan the sparse pockets of tungsten embedded within. At the high springs along the mountain crest, you can still see the broken rock, pounded into small pieces by a Kelly for panning.

Lon Kelly was a man who liked to be left alone. He had asked for little from life except an opportunity to work. His last years were spent in frustration and bafflement. Forced by circumstances to seek old age assistance, he had no proof of his existence—no birth record, no voting record. He'd been married in a foreign country. He'd never been counted by a census taker. Nothing! He was here, alive. Anyone could see that he was old. By his thinking this visual evidence should have been enough. Even the most doubting should be convinced by this. Not so with the government. That's not the way they operate. If you're not part of some musty record, you just ain't. Moving, breathing, eating, functioning, occupying space, that doesn't mean a thing to them. You have to be a statistic or else you don't exist.

Jim was the first of the remaining Kellys to go—gut shot, lifted out of his saddle by a slug from one of those old guns made for buffalo. With a temper more fiery than his brothers, his life had been one of violence. He who had lived by the gun died by the gun. I remember that shot. It came at supper time. My Dad and I were across the table from one another. For an incredibly long time, like thunder, it rumbled and echoed through the craggy canyons of the steep mountain backdrop. "Gun or dynamite blast?", we wondered aloud. Next morning a cowboy rode up canyon to tell us Jim was dead, the assailant jailed. I can close my eyes and once more hear that rumbling reverberation off the mountain. Those were innocent years, impressionable years. I hadn't been to war yet. It was the first shot I ever heard that took a life.

Lon and John didn't last many years longer. The Kellys were gone from the mountain. With the inflow of newcomers, there aren't too many people around who knew of their existence. The hikers and the backpackers, who have invaded the once seldom-used mountain trails, pass by with no inkling of Will's lonely grave amid the peaks. Perhaps it's better so. The brothers were essentially loners. They didn't cater much to strangers. Wouldn't have appreciated this latter day influx. It is fitting that one of them wasn't carted off to town for burial. If the Huachucas ever belonged to anyone, it was the Kellys. I'm glad Will's up there keeping an eye on their mountains. "Guard them well 'Old Timer'. I, too, love those once lonely peaks."

WILL KELLY'S GRAVE

I paused one day some rest to seek
On the snowshed side of a lofty peak.
Before me lay Will Kelly's grave,
And to his life some thought I gave.

Now poor Will Kelly, so they say,
Froze to death one winter day
In his lonely cabin among the pine,
Built on the edge of his tungsten mine.

No one had seen Will for a spell.
He could be sick or he could have fell.
Worried were his neighbors down below,
A trail they broke through the waist deep snow.

They found Will Kelly there in his bed.
He was very cold and he was very dead.
A muttered prayer for the sake of his soul,
They buried poor Will in his prospect hole.

So I sat there very sad and still
Had life been kind to you poor Will?
Not always were you alone and old
In your ramshackled shack in the bitter cold.

Raging River, Lonely Trail

Once you were a carefree boy
Filled with laughter, filled with joy,
Each morning to a glowing world awoke
In your family home at Kelly's Oak.

But boyhood slips so fast away,
Work comes hard on the heels of play.
Youth is gone before you know
You've headed south for Mexico.

By a wagon piled with fresh cut pine
Destined for a booming copper mine,
Plodding along with the oxen slow,
From these mountains you did go.

Never one to hedge or shirk
You reveled in the mine's hard work,
Sweet music rang the hammer's sound
As you drove the drill steel in the ground.

After day's work comes the night
Laughter gay, eyes flashing bright.
Fiery liquor with after-glow,
All seems well in Mexico.

But revolution comes with grim despair,
No longer are you welcome there.
By the dark of night you set forth,
Hiding by night on your journey north.

A life's work gone but still alive
At your old home you did arrive
To take up a prospector's lonely ways
And live out your remaining days.

So old timer, when next I sit
By your crude grave to rest a bit
And marvel at the far off view
As I'm sure in your time you did too—

Vaughn Short

Then once again I'll wish you well,
So many things that you could tell
About living here on mountain high
While down below the world rushed by.

And though hardships came your way
If you could speak I'm sure you'd say
That you loved these mountains best.
No better place for your final rest.

Now, friend, if ever this grave you seek
On the snowshed side of some lofty peak,
Remember that though Will Kelly's gone
His love for these mountains lingers on.

And if you are inclined to pray
Then bow your head and kind words say
For the soul of a man whose wants were few,
Who did the things that he had to do.

Long hours he toiled in his little mine
In a hard rock ledge 'neath towering pine.
Though arduous the work with little pay,
He dug his own grave before he passed away.

"Then his niche in life he found"

The motors are disappearing from the boats on the white water rivers. You can see the trend. Each year more and more parties are rowing. This means smaller boats, fewer people to the boat, and consequently more boatmen. Many of these oarsmen are young, college boys rowing for the thrill and the hell of it—real physical specimens with lots of macho.

I started this poem about boatmen with an entirely different direction and ending in mind, even a different title. I wrote four verses and there it set for a couple of years. When I picked it up again, it came out the way it is now. In no way am I trying to imply that all boatmen are like the stud in the poem. On the other hand, of all those young fellows you see stroking down the river, one or two could easily fit the pattern.

The Macho Boatman

On the campus was a real live wire,
Joe College at his best.
A going guy—a ball of fire
He stood above the rest.

From his flowing locks to his sandaled feet,
To the muscles that bulged in his arms,
He considered himself a rare, rare treat,
A super stud of endless charms.

When he shucked his shirt to get a tan
The chicks all turned in awe
To view this wonderful hunk of man,
And they all liked what they saw.

Out in the street at a pick-up game
He was always captain of the team.
Flocking in the girls all came
To eyeball this living dream.

And as he breezed through college,
This stud with awesome looks
Had gained a lot of knowledge
That wasn't taught in books.

In campus life there comes a day,
A day out in late spring,
That marks the end of fun and games.
Now it's time to do your thing.

As every boat is launched to sea
It's sails must be unfurled,
Thus even living Gods set free,
Must face the cruel, cold world.

Out there it's a different life.
It's humdrum at the best.
The days are full of toil and strife,
The nights are meant for rest.

Most will trudge to work each day
And home again each night.
Twice a month they'll draw their pay
And pretend their future's bright.

In time many will go down.
The system they'll not buck.
In dim-lit bars they'll try to drown
Their damnable bad luck.

But our hero's a cat of another breed,
He's just not made the same.
He will not play their game of greed,
Or live out his life this tame.

Raging River, Lonely Trail

There's bound to be another way,
A way much more fulfilling.
Still a chance to laugh and play
And lead a life more thrilling.

Even though his schooling's done
He's learned a lot of tricks.
So why not have a life of fun,
Still make it with the chicks.

Now his niche in life he's found,
He couldn't ask for more.
Once again the girls flock 'round
His torso to adore.

For now his time he does devote
To running water white,
Through rapids rough, at oar of boat
He does display his might.

"Drain down that stagnant pond"

One day while sorting through slides, I ran across some that were taken the day the pickets walked, protesting water under Rainbow Bridge. One picture caught my eye. It was Clair Quist of Moki Mac Expeditions. He looked every bit the protester. Hollywood couldn't have cast a better one—floppy leather hat, long shaggy hair, fierce black beard, and then there was the sign. In large spray-can letters it stated, "REOPEN THE WATER GATES." Of course that was the purpose of the picket thing, to get the level of the lake pulled down. Clair and his sign said it all and very well. He stoutly insists the only poetry he ever wrote was on restroom walls, but I have to give him credit for the following little poem. I just looked at the picture and wrote the words. His sign was doing the talking.

A rondeau is written to a very strict formula. I'm not a disciplined enough writer to follow fixed formulas, but this one just seemed to fall into place.

Open the Gates

Open the gates and let them flow!
A rushing let the water go.
Drain down that stagnant pond!
Let's think of the future and on beyond.
There may never be another Rainbow.

For nature's ways are very slow,
Aeons to build a bridge, you know,
Of the one we have we're very fond.
Open the gates!

Centuries of rain and the wind must blow,
Ice in the seams and the melting snow
All chip away at the sandstone's bond
And still the rock may not respond.
Another bridge may never grow.
Open the gates!

"What better place than a mountain top"

The following poem is a letter I once sent, one of those kind where you talk into a recorder and then mail the cassette. I was going through a very moody time and it reflects in the verse. On a pack trip into Grand Gulch, a mule had taken a dive over a bluff. I didn't disengage myself fast enough, so when the knot on the end of the lead rope went through my hand it did a job on a finger—one of those tendon and joint deals. Now a finger isn't too big of an appendage, but it can hurt. During the reconstruction months I wasn't clocking the sleep I needed. My light and breezy outlook wasn't always there. Like a sore-pawed old bear, I wanted to be out of sight, out of hearing, crawl into some reassuring familiar lair and lick my wounds. That's what took me atop the Huachuca (Waa-choo-ca) Mountains.

I came to the Huachucas to live at the age of sixteen. I couldn't go back to that dilapidated old cabin where I had spent so many happy years. The Forest Service had seen to that. At one time there were a number of cabins scattered in high remote areas of the mountain, many of them log. Some dated back to before the turn of the century. It was decreed by powers within the Forest Service that they shouldn't be allowed to crumble into a dignified death. Under a scorched earth policy, the torch was applied. Some of the most majestic trees in the mountains died when these cabins burned. Crumpled tin, twisted bedstead, and charred tree stumps remained, a very sad and sorry sight. Enough of that.

The Huachucas are very near and dear to me. In the steep-brush-tangled canyons, away from the trails, there are forgotten places that only I know about. Places I discovered when I was a kid. Not long before this book went to press, a devastating fire swept the mountains. What now remains I do not know. As yet I haven't had the heart to return for a look. Man had long misused the mountains. The old timers took the big trees. The slopes grew back in thick brush. The no burn policy of the protecting agencies did not allow nature to police it. Then came drought, a careless camper, and Mother Nature in vengeful mood supplied the hot, dry winds for a holocaust.

I thought a lot, that day, sitting atop my special mountains. Thoughts of the old times. I looked far across at the Chiricahua (Cheer-i-cow-wa) Mountains, my birthplace. I recalled the strange little country kid who had grown up there. On my third birthday my mother had a party for me. I remember it well. Most everyone was older than I. One of my gifts was a brilliant red necktie, and I was ecstatic. It was one of the highlights of my young life. In later years, I didn't dude it up much, never had much use for neckties. As a dandy, I guess I peaked early.

Nearer than the Chiricahuas to my lofty perch, were the Mule Mountains cradling the town of Bisbee with its copper mines. There I'd learned what hard work was all about. It occurred to me I'd spent my entire life within a hundred miles of my viewpoint, excepting of course visits, vacations, wars, and such. One at a time, I reviewed the visible mountain ranges, and there are many. I tried to recall the first visit, the last visit, and some of the times in between. With some, my relationship had been casual, with others intimate. Last I came to the Baboquivaries (Baa-boe-key-ver-ees). Pete Cowgill, who writes, once climbed Babo and found religious tracts tucked into the register. He wrote, "Don't preach to me on mountain tops." Ed Abbey who also wields the pen followed. He liked Pete's sentiment. Liked it well enough to put it into a book. I pondered and I had to agree. No one should invade that intimacy which exists between climber and mountain. But on the other hand, where would one find a more lofty pulpit? Where could the thoughts be more pure? As long as you restricted your congregation to yourself, I decided preaching would be permissible.

The day wore on and the shadows lengthened, I turned to my recorder. I had correspondence long overdue.

Did you ever notice how other people's letters always seem more interesting? I guess it's the snoop in us. Anyway, The letter: Oh, by the way! When my wife first heard this poem she thought I ought to call it, *Sexy Heaven*.

Vaughn Short

Musing on a Mountain

I'm sitting here on lonely peak
Where the trees one sided grow.
They've been dwarfed by howling wind
Their trunks twisted by heavy snow.

And yet this day is calm—serene
Though summer's already passed this way
But there's some pleasant times still left
Before cold weather's here to stay.

Far below the grass—no longer green.
Beyond lie hills, barren, gray and red.
Leafless the cottonwoods on far San Pedro's banks,
Pale ghosts of a season dead.

Long before the Pilgrims landed—
Through this valley below—Coronado came,
Casting long shadows o'er the land.
This forest bears his name.

Looking up, mare's-tails in a sky of blue,
Maybe it's good I came today.
Chances are I won't be back
'Til winter's had its say.

For it seems the fires of youth
No longer burn so bright.
Where I used to laugh at cold and snow,
Now I seek my bed at night.

The view today—a good hundred miles.
Within the radius of this scan
My life has ticked off day by day
On a clock with a yearly hand.

Raging River, Lonely Trail

This is a place I've often came
In other years—years long ago—
I'd watch the daytime shadows creep,
Then I'd dream by my campfire's glow.

There are bits of charcoal still about
Perhaps campfire remnants of my youth
When a starry-eyed kid sat and dreamed
Oblivious to the cold hard truth.

But no longer do I fool myself.
Those days have long since past.
And somehow it's better so,
It's good that youth doesn't last.

So my clock of time it says past noon
And my own life's shadows creep.
What better place than a mountain top
To ponder the mysteries deep?

Do I believe there is a heaven?
Honestly, really, I do not know.
But the stereotypes I've always heard
No way, man! No way can they be so.

Does the miracle of mind just disappear?
Nature wastes nothing, so this I can't see.
But where it goes and what it does
That's way beyond the likes of me.

Peering into the dark abyss ahead
Some day—We all must reach the brink.
If I could vision a life beyond
This is what I'd like to think:

That somewhere out amid the stars,
Somewhere out in outer space.
Far beyond this world of ours
There'd be this very special place—

Vaughn Short

A spot to rest in long sought peace,
No rigid rules, no frantic pace,
A haven for tranquility and love
A place where lonely souls embrace.

And if this place should be for real,
When two souls with compassion intermesh,
I'd like to think you still could feel
The silk of skin—the warmth of flesh,

The caress of hair—the seeking lips
The whispering breath of tender sigh
The turn of breast—the flare of hips
The soft and yield of inner thigh

Sweet trembling love—the lingering kiss
Gone the loneliness—no longing need—
A fountain of eternal bliss—
Only love here, no place for greed.

No cutting words—no need for fear—
A place where spirit could soar and fly
There'd be no trivial bickering here—
A place where even men could cry.

Tucked away in celestial skies,
Concealed where the petty cannot find
Let them have their own spot faraway
This for only those of tender mind.

Sitting here on mountain top
My sermonette I've preached.
And even the dreamer in me must know
It's a goal that will never be reached.

But if I was in the preaching trade
I'd forget those streets of gold
And angels whanging away on harps,
My religion would be easier sold.

Raging River, Lonely Trail

The air's turned chill and my jacket's on,
But still I can feel the bite
And even if I had my pack
I'm in no mood to spend the night.

The trail down is rough and steep
A hundred miles of asphalt lies ahead.
Home, hearth, and love, they beckon strong
So I leave soon for my bed.

But I'll be back, I have no doubts,
When days lengthen again in spring,
This is a pilgrimage of sorts,
My own very special thing.

                        Good night

"I thought of only you my dear"

If you are married—WOW!—is it ever easy to get into trouble. People who wouldn't know you if they met you on the street can get you in hot water without even trying. That's what John Denver did to me. Now I have nothing against John. Even drove all the way to Phoenix to see his concert one time, but he did get me in trouble. Seems he wrote, "Annie's Song." Wrote it for his wife and a darn good song it is too.

"How come?", my wife said one day. The words, "How come?" are usually a forerunner to problems around our house. "How come, John Denver writes pretty songs for his wife and you have never written one thing for me?" See how easily trouble can slip up on you? See what that guy Denver did to me? After stumbling and stuttering around trying to come up with some plausible excuse, I sat down to write. I really wish the poem had turned out better. I'm just not a pressure writer. Someday I'll get around to writing the real one for her, the one I'd like to write. One as good as "Annie's Song"—a masterpiece! In the meantime, now that the heat's off, I have all these ideas. Ideas for lots of other poems, real super ideas that I just pave to get on paper.

OF YOU MY DEAR

I've stood on the deck in southern seas
And felt the salt spray in the breeze.
I've lain 'neath the sun's soothing balm
On sandy beach beneath swaying palm,
And I thought of only you, my dear.
My thoughts were of only you.

I've basked by campfire's warming glow
And watched the driftwood burn down low,
While the air crept in cold and still,
Until I huddled from the chill,
And I thought of only you, my love,
My thoughts were of only you.

On mountain top at break of day,
Dim were the ranges far away
As I gazed out o'er the valleys wide
Wishing that you were by my side.
For I longed for only you, my sweet.
I longed for only you.

Amid the rush of crowded street
Alone, no friendly face to greet,
Ill at ease, wishing to be far away
But thoughts of you would save my day.
For I felt you very near, sweetheart.
I felt you very near.

"What are your thoughts, Kathy, my dear"

    I've sat around a lot of campfires and acknowledged requests for poems from people within the circle. Only once have I ever had a request to compose one.

    I have a friend who lives in an east coast state. I trekked with him in the canyons of the Escalante some years back. He has a friend, Kathy, who lives in California. He first met her on a trip he had taken to Alaska. My east coast friend, searching for a Christmas gift for Kathy, decided a poem would be nice. I don't know how many poets are listed in the yellow pages? Perhaps none! I've never looked under the classification. Maybe my friend didn't either. Anyway, out in Arizona I received a letter wanting to know if I would write the poem. This was somewhat of a challenge. There are many things that might turn a poet on: an injustice, a heroic act, a romantic tryst, a lover's moon, a beautiful lady, a serene canyon, a misty mountain, and the list is long. To be confronted with little more than a name is something else. How could I write of golden curls and blue eyes? The lady might be a brunette. Some flaxen-haired beauty might not appreciate raven locks. I was faced with a lot of limitations. I did have one valuable piece of knowledge—Kathy liked the outdoors—so on this I based the poem. I mailed it to the east coast for its long journey back out west. A well-traveled bit of verse, indeed. It was fun trying to meet the challenge. I hope Kathy didn't mind being written about by a stranger. I hope she liked the poem. It is my understanding that it was engraved on a plaque by an artist.

Kathy

Kathy stood by the lonely sea
And the wind was in her hair.
The waves dashed in so wild and free
And salt spray filled the air.

"Why so still, Kathy, my dear?
Why do you linger so long?
Does the wind whisper in your ear?
Does the sea sing a secret song?"

Kathy sat on a greening peak
Watching the frail flowers blow.
Busy bees played hide and seek
As they darted to and fro.

"What are your thoughts, Kathy, my dear?
Why sit on this mountain crest?
Do the bees hum something only you hear?
Is it a song of peace and rest?"

Kathy sat by a river's edge
In a far off northern land
And with a twig she traced a pledge
In the smooth surface of the sand.

"What did you write, Kathy; my dear?
What did you scribe with a twig?
Was it something for all to revere?
Was it something momentous and big?"

"Oh I linger long by the lonely sea
For the air smells sweet and clean,
And I sit there on the mountain top
For the world's so fresh and green."

"And what I wrote in the clean wet sand
On that Arctic river's edge,
Was to enjoy this life and just be me.
That was my solemn pledge!"

"Those were the things that were whispered to me"

Grand Gulch is a canyon of many moods. I have personally experienced a few. Within its depths I have seen a downpour of rain send the silty, red waterfalls plummeting over the high cliffs. I have leaned into icy gales, and felt the driven snow upon my face. At times, the sun beat relentlessly upon the dry canyon bottom, and I dug for water to drink.

Whatever the whim of the Gulch, whatever fare it might bestow upon you, it is an intriguing place. The high cliff dwellings are fascinating, the rock art unbelievable. The paintings and carvings on the walls offer something for everyone. If you can't find a drawing on the rock that you can identify with, then good friend, I don't think you looked very hard. Pictured there are game animals for the hunter, snakes for the herpetologist, birds for the good Audubon people, a humped back flute player for the musician, corn for the farmer, pregnant girls for careless lovers, masks for thespians, old arthritic men, and the list goes on and on.

If you really love the old Gulch, and sit alone on some moonlit night, gazing upward at the crumbling, high-perched homes, wondering how it might have been, then perhaps those friendly folk of long ago will drop around for a neighborly chat.

The Old Grand Gulch at Night

Once when the moon hung big and round
In the old Grand Gulch at night,
Eerie the shadows on the ground,
Uncanny was the light.

High in the cliffs where the old ones dwelt
Ancient spirits rose and stirred.
They crowded about, their presence I felt,
Then their whispered words I heard.

They told of when the corn maids danced
While the drummers beat and swayed.
Around and around they wheeled and pranced
While the humped-back fluter played.

Those were the days when life was good,
When there was time to sit and dream
While the soft winds played in the cottonwood
And the beavers dammed the stream.

Vaughn Short

When gold the squash lay on the ground,
Corn leaves rustled in the breeze,
And all about game did abound.
And there were song birds in the trees.

These are the things that were whispered to me
In the old Grand Gulch that night,
Not of the droughts or the misery
Of survival's struggling fight.

So when I look high on the wall
And the crumbling ruins I see,
Then is the time that I recall
What the spirits said to me.

Then I feel the drummer's beat,
Hear the humped-back fluter play,
See the dancing girls on nimble feet
As they circle, prance, and sway.

This to me is what the old Gulch means
When I sit down here below.
And I know they're true, these ancient scenes,
For the old ones told me so.

Raging River, Lonely Trail

"On a lucky try at water low"

This is a rather facetious poem about a boat going through Lava Falls. In no way is it intended to portray the grandeur of that awesome rapid. I don't believe anyone could paint a true word picture of Lava. You have to stand on the edge and feel your stomach sink. Waiting at the top of the falls, knowing that in a few minutes you're going to be down in that raging water, it's not too different from those last moments before going into combat. It's a rapid that makes even the biggest rafts look small.

LAVA FALLS

Now there rages a rapid wild
Lava Falls is its name.
One mad ride upon its waves.
And you'll never be the same.

Deep they say still water flows,
But it isn't half the fun
As that which boils, heaves, and churns
Down this rock strewn run.

To Lava came a limp old raft,
Surplus from World War Two.
On a lucky try at water low
It once had made it through.

Vaughn Short

It paused there upon the brink
With apprehension, fear, and doubt.
Could it survive that awesome plunge?
Last chance to chicken out!

No matter how the water churns,
No matter how wild the ride,
This is no time for turning back
For there's such a thing as pride.

So down into the surging falls
Eased the ancient boat.
The heaving torrent gathered it in
Now it's sink or float.

How this old raft will heave and plunge.
Turn, tumble, toss, and spin,
But even if it makes it through
It can really never win.

For if it ever comes once more
To pause there on the brink,
There'll always be that nagging doubt,
It still could flip or sink!

Raging River, Lonely Trail

"To really pass the test supreme"

It's found in the curricula of colleges. Among Boy Scouts it's a big thing. Bookstores carry numerous volumes on the subject. Clubs for little old ladies have experts lecture on it. Some people even go out and try it. I'm talking about wilderness survival. "Desert Survival," they call it here in our arid Southwest.

Among my friends are many who I'm sure could pull it off. At times I have given thoughts to living off the country, but it's the rules and regulations that turn me off. If you can't be as free as the coyote to take what's available, then it's a farce. That wily fellow goes where the food is. If I was lunching on some unappetizing weed, it would be hard to convince my taste buds that I was doing my best, when I knew there was an orchard or a garden within a day's hike. How much enthusiasm could a person have for a meal of creepies and crawlies when three months' supply of jerky was placidly chewing its cud nearby. There are just too many no-nos. That's what dampens my ardor. Oh, if you want to go out and eat lizards, bugs, and snakes, that's great. Everyone for his own thing. Like my friend, Bill, in the poem, if I ever go out to take a survival test, I hope to do a bit better.

The little gimmicks that could mean so much in a starving situation, I learned early from my mother. I suppose that is the natural succession of learning. It's the mother lion who teaches her cubs to hunt. In earlier times, although the man was considered the provider, the woman did a lot toward putting food on the table. It was the woman who went out with the forked stick and twisted the rabbit out of its burrow. A handy woman could take a whole covey of quail in her wire-net trap with little fuss or bother. My mother taught my brother and I how to whittle out a figure-four trigger when we were very small. This trigger can make a deadfall out of a log, or scaled down, it can be set under a box and take small creatures unharmed. It's good on anything from mice to moose. I've never had any occasion to use it to get food, but garrisoned in the Philippines, I was an exterminator of rats. We were plagued with these huge, marauding rodents. Placing the trigger beneath one end of an army footlocker, I sent many a rat to that place beyond. I acquired somewhat of a mountain man image in that outfit. Trap a rat and become a mountain man. Flip in your graves, old timers. How times do change.

Anyway, it's all the talk about survival that brought about this story of Bill. If you are ever bit by the survival bug, and take out for the hills, I wish you the best of luck. If you decide to go for the doctorate, to take the supreme test, remember poor Bill. *BE CAUTIOUS!*

THE BALLAD OF BARE-ASS BILL

Once there was a fellow—
A real ordinary sort of guy—
Who sort of loafed through life
And watched the world go by.

And what went on in old Bill's head,
Some of it was kind of strange,
But he wasn't scheming to get well known
Or make a pile of change.

Sometimes he'd sit within a bar
And bend his elbow a bit.
Many people shook their heads,
But old Bill didn't give a whit.

Some folks thought that he was dumb,
And others that he might be wise.
He was really sort of in between,
Not a complete dud, and yet no prize.

Now Bill had a deep down feeling
That catastrophe with death and fear
Might send the old world reeling,
And he felt that time was near.

Raging River, Lonely Trail

If the people lost their goodies,
Their cars and boats and planes,
There were no guns left to shoot with,
No more railroads, no more trains.

If the buildings were all tumbled,
The electricity no longer flowed—
There was no more central heating,
No warm beds when it snowed.

Then Bill he had misgivings
About those sitting up on top.
Could they lead and feed the people?
Or would things come to a stop?

Those sitting in paneled offices
With their votes, mandates, and such,
When it came down to nitty gritty
Would they really amount to much?

Just some regular, average fellow
With some common sense and hustle
Might do a hell of a better job
Than all that political muscle.

Bill felt that if the world went "BOOM,"
And he lucked out and was alive,
He'd have the savvy to lend a hand
And help the rest survive.

Oh, he didn't figure to lead the nation,
But if things were leveled to the ground
He could help his friends and neighbors
'Til a new life could be found.

One day in his favorite bar,
After he'd tossed down a few,
Bill reached the big decision
Of what he had to do.

Vaughn Short

For if destiny had marked him
To be a savior of man,
He'd better be able to produce
And come up with a plan.

He needed some credentials.
He had to have some proof
That he'd be the one to follow,
Else the folks might be aloof.

So old Bill gave some thought
To a real convincing test
To prove to the most doubting
That he stood above the rest.

The way to show he could get by
Without all those gadgets and frills
Was to depart from civilization
And dwell out in the hills.

But if he was gone a month or two
And came back sleek and trim,
Would it really mean much
If he took a gun with him?

Many could go out in the wilds
And for a time survive.
But would it really prove a lot,
Them coming back alive?

For there would be a lot of yokels
Who could cling to this old life
If they took along some matches,
String, fish-hooks, and a knife.

Then Bill had a great idea,
One to remove all doubt.
It would sway the most doubting.
He swore to try it out.

To really pass the test supreme,
And this might shock some prude,
He'd have to start out naked,
In the altogether, bare-assed nude!

If from such a meager start
He could garner food to eat,
Then all would have to admit
He'd accomplished quite a feat.

Next morning he rolled out of bed
And took a lonely trail
Far into the distant hills.
He swore he wouldn't fail.

For this meant a lot to him,
He was a dedicated man.
He bade civilization a fond adieu
'Til he'd carried out his plan.

He stopped out in the desert,
Said, "This will be the spot!
Here I'll prove to one and all
If I'm man enough or not."

Then old Bill dropped his clothes,
He'd never felt so free.
He flapped around and danced about
And shouted out in glee!

"This is the way to live," he cried,
"Without restricting clothes.
When I return I'll spread the word
Until everybody knows!"

Then he gathered up those useless duds
Wrapped them in a bundle tight.
With his one and only match,
He gave those rags a light.

Vaughn Short

"Now," he said, "I've done it.
I've cut the binding ties.
No man knows if he can make it
'Til he gets out here and tries."

Chuck full of confidence
He laughed like it was a joke
As the flames leaped ever higher,
And his clothes went up in smoke.

Naked and alone he stood
Out in the great outdoors.
He had no responsibilities.
No job, no tedious chores.

But freedom has its drawbacks,
Nature boys still must eat.
As hunger pangs beset him
He set out to find a treat.

Lizards and bugs were all about,
Bill didn't want to stoop so low.
A fellow should do better
If he was really in the know.

He'd like himself a venison chop,
That kind of meal he'd love.
He'd even compromise a bit
Settle for quail or breast of dove.

Then he had sober reflections,
He knew it would be tough.
He'd have to postpone that meal,
For a while it would be rough.

Starting out from scratch,
It wasn't going to be easy.
But he wouldn't take to eating bugs,
His stomach was too queasy.

Sure he'd get real hungry,
With that he could cope,
Until he got some tools made—
Then he'd have some hope.

A greenhorn he was not.
He'd been a country boy.
There were plenty of little tricks
He'd be able to employ.

Birds were easy prey to trap.
He knew how to make the sets,
But with no store to buy supplies
He'd have to weave the nets.

He'd have to seek a boggy spring
To find the slender reeds,
Then he could weave the traps
To take care of his needs.

Now Bill knew a dandy trap
For taking animals large or small.
It was easiest of all to make—
That reliable old deadfall.

But he would proceed step by step
Before his plans got bigger.
He couldn't set a deadfall
'Til he'd whittled out a trigger.

So the thing he needed most
In his newfangled life
Was an instrument to cut with.
He'd have to make a knife.

First the knife, then the trap,
Then perchance he'd get a doe,
Then he'd have some likely sinew
To string himself a bow.

He'd have to keep a hustling,
For summer was almost gone.
He'd need a lot of furry skins
With winter coming on.

He also had to look about,
'Cause when he got some meat to cook,
He needed implements to build a fire—
He knew just what it took!

Methodically he started out—
He was one ingenious cuss.
At first he suffered hardships,
But he never made a fuss.

The sun burned his tender skin.
He had to seek the shade.
Sitting there he chipped at stone
Until his tools were made.

Then he trapped the animals—
Only what he needed to survive.
He called them his bank account—
Those he left alive.

Soon his skin grew dark and tough,
The sun did him little harm.
But he gathered furs for winter
When he needed to be warm.

Then the winter came and went.
Old Bill made it through.
Spring was an easy season,
There wasn't much to do.

Now the plants were growing,
Plenty there was to eat.
Young animals were easy prey
When he needed him some meat.

"I've made it through the worst," he said
"To stay longer there's no reason.
I've proved that I can survive
No matter what the season."

"I've been out here a goodly spell.
I've suffered quite a bit,
But I have made my point—
There's no denying it."

"Should disaster ever strike,
Although may God forbid,
People will have to turn to me
Because of what I did."

"Now it's time that I went back.
My experiment is through.
I have proven to myself
What I really always knew."

"That I had the know how,
The cunning and the stealth,
To live off Mother Nature
And still maintain my health."

"It hasn't been too easy,
Its been a big ordeal.
But I'm glad I made the sacrifice—
That is how I feel."

Bill took a look about.
His possessions they were few.
When he prepared to leave
There wasn't much to do.

He gathered up an old deer hide,
It didn't smell so good.
But he had to go back looking
As decent as he could.

Vaughn Short

Oh, he liked that good free feeling
Of living in the raw,
But people in civilization
Were particular about what they saw.

The deer hide folks would understand.
Bill just knew they would.
He'd get himself proper clothing
As quickly as he could.

Then he thought it over.
It wouldn't seem too right
To barge in the way he looked.
He'd better go at night.

So as darkness lowered,
Bill came creeping in.
The town dogs got a whiff
And set up a mighty din.

For Bill had a powerful smell
Wrapped in that old deer hide,
But he wasn't about to drop it,
He had this foolish pride.

He'd set out to prove to people
He could be fed and fully clothed.
He wasn't going to drop that skin,
Though the smelly thing he loathed.

The dogs grew ever bolder,
Shrill and loud the bark.
They snapped, snarled, and bit at Bill
'Til he fled out through the dark.

He tried to avoid them,
But it was all in vain.
They ferociously set upon him
'Til he screamed out in pain.

Doors were flung wide open
As old Bill thundered by—
A pack of dogs upon his heels
Baying in full cry.

A woman screamed, "Go away,
You dirty, creepy bum!
This is a decent town.
We don't want any filthy scum!"

Someone yelled, "Stop you thief."
A gun blazed in the night
To poor befuddled, speeding Bill'
It didn't seem quite right.

He'd had the best intentions
To help the people of this town,
But they showed no appreciation.
They'd really let him down.

Poor Bill's lungs were bursting.
His breath was running out.
Still those dogs snapped and bit
And circled all about.

As he began to despair
Of ever breaking free,
Looming in the dark ahead,
He spied a big old tree.

Agile as any monkey
He scrambled to the top.
The baying dogs circled 'round,
They didn't want to stop.

So Bill sat on his lofty perch
And waited for the dawn
When he hoped those yelping dogs
Would shut up and move on.

Vaughn Short

Time he had to ponder,
He made up his mind.
He'd forsake civilization,
He'd leave it all behind.

A curse on all the people
They were no good, cheap, and crummy!
All he'd done was try to help,
They'd played him for a dummy.

He'd return to the free life.
The hills would be his home,
Where the air was fit for breathing,
And room there was to roam.

If some unwelcome stranger
Ever wandered near Bill's lair,
Then he would go in hiding.
Didn't want him in his hair.

From this day henceforward
His own business he would mind.
He'd buddy with the coyotes.
To hell with his own kind!

So he left behind civilization,
And the thought never occurred
That he had made a big mistake.
He remained true to his word.

And as the years rolled by
He came to love the simple life,
And he lived without the pressures,
Without the stress and the strife.

He tried to keep his distance
From any passerby.
Didn't want any human contact.
Didn't even want to try.

The longer that he lived apart
The wilder he did look.
For some kind of hairy monster
He easily could be mistook.

Sometimes unwary strangers,
Out wandering in the hills,
Would glimpse the fleeing wildman.
They really got their thrills.

A hunter threw away his gun.
Back to camp he ran,
"I just spied myself a demon,
An abominable cactus man!"

Into town a prospector came,
Bent really out of shape
He'd seen a terrible monster—
Half human and half ape.

Tales were told and legends grew
As time did swiftly pass.
Most forgot about old Bill,
They called this man, "Bare-ass."

For Bill had returned to nature,
Clothes he did not wear.
Except for winter's icy blasts
He always traveled bare.

Nine-feet tall he stood,
That's what the people said.
His arms hung down below his knees
And his eyes were blazing red.

They swore he left a track
Twice the size of man.
Two long yards between each stride.
Whatever he turned and ran.

So old Bare-ass' fame it grew
Until it spread far and wide.
Local people liked to brag,
And looked on him with pride.

Some thought he should be hunted down,
Stuffed for the courthouse hall.
Others thought this a bit too much
Maybe just his head upon the wall.

But people who remembered back
Said, "There's no need to kill.
He may be screwy in the head
But it's only old harmless Bill."

A stranger came to town one day
Different from the rest—
Bowler hat and big cigar,
Gold chain across his chest.

He pounded loud upon the bar
Announced for all to hear.
"Listen to this proposition.
It will pay you very dear."

"A thousand bucks I have
For the man who can produce
Alive and without any harm
This creature running loose."

"For the patrons of my carnival,
Good money they will spend,
To step into a sideshow
To view your hairy friend."

Among those sippers of the suds,
Old drinking pals of Bill's,
They forgot he'd been a buddy
Before he defected to the hills.

Raging River, Lonely Trail

Without a thought of old times
They groveled in their greed
To pocket a thousand dollars,
They had this burning need.

So there was a scramble
To catch the wild man first.
The drinkers stampeded for the door.
They pushed and shoved and cursed.

Those rough and rugged four-wheelers
Were the first to leave the town.
They left with wheels a spinning,
And throttles pushed way down.

To be the first one there—
That seemed their only plan.
They lurched across the desert,
Each certain of his man.

Sitting high on a rugged butte,
Where no vehicle could ever go,
Bill sat in puzzled amazement
And watched the chaos down below.

They crisscrossed and circled 'round
'Til the gas was running out,
Then those tired, discouraged off-roaders
Began to have some doubt.

Some vowed to return
To try another day,
But in time they all gave up.
This just was not the way.

There were those who rode on horseback,
They were later on the scene.
They came with dogs a trailing,
Hounds, cold-nosed and mean.

Vaughn Short

Now Bill remembered well the dogs.
He found them very scary.
He knew he'd better be on the ball,
Be alert and ever wary.

So the days went by,
The dogs bayed and chased the deer.
Bill remained ever cautious.
Not once did they get near.

After the horsemen came the trappers,
Men with crazy far out dreams.
They brought all kinds of contraptions
To implement their schemes.

There were peculiar looking cages
Equipped with triggers and trap doors,
And they left the strangest baits
Placed upon the floors.

Old Bill would stealthily sneak in
Under the light of stars,
With a stick he'd spear the beefsteaks,
Pilfer away the candy bars.

He loved to rob these fancy traps,
It was an easy way to eat.
He enjoyed the game he was playing,
Looked forward to each night's treat.

But he remained ever wary.
It would be disastrous to get bold.
One night he got a real prize—
A Playboy centerfold.

So the trappers and the horsemen
And those who drove the bouncing cars,
One by one they grew discouraged
And went back to the bars.

But one who sought old Bare-ass
Was shrewder than the rest.
He scoffed at all their contraptions.
His plan was far the best.

He said, "I'll bring the old boy back
Without those fancy traps with lures.
All I need's a little luck,
And a good supply of Coors."

"To trap is serious business.
You can't treat it like a whim.
Whatever animal you go for,
You must think the same as them."

"I will go out on the desert—
This wild man I will find.
The rest should be easy
For I think I know his mind.' '

"Now I knew old Bare-ass
Back when they called him Bill.
I think I had the old boy pegged,
And I bet I know him still."

"Bill's always had a failing.
With a weakness he's been cursed.
He loves to toss the beer down
He has one hellacious thirst."

"The solution to my problem,
If I'm going to bring Bill in,
Is to take a good supply of beer,
Get him drinking once again."

So he set out for the hills
Looking for a track.
If he could find old Bill's sign,
He knew he'd bring him back.

He camped out in the desert.
He played a waiting game,
Somewhere he knew old Bare-ass
Was doing much the same.

Old Bill would be suspicious,
Of that he had no doubt.
There'd been way too much traffic
Trying to flush him out.

The thing was not to hurry,
A thousand was a lot of dough.
For that kind of money,
He could afford to take it slow.

Old Bare-ass would make a slip,
When? He could only wonder.
Sooner or later it had to come.
Bill would make a stupid blunder.

Camped one night by a water hole,
This stalker heard a dry twig crack.
Next morning in the mud
There was a naked track.

"Now," he said, "I've got him.
The delivery date is near,
For the elusive wild man
Is lurking close to here."

"I'll take it very easy.
No need now to rush,
For my good nose tells me,
Old Bare-ass is hiding in the brush."

"I don't want to scare him off,
So I won't get too near,
But here in a conspicuous spot
I'll leave a can of beer."

"I know old Bill's seen bad times.
But he's suffered through the worst.
He'll soon be in a nice snug cage
He can't deny his thirst."

"With one can I'll not tease him—
No way would that be right—
So on that distant hilltop
I 'll set another, still in sight."

"Now if I know my man,
After two cans of brew,
He's not going to want to stop
'Til he's tossed down quite a few."

"So I'll just string them out
From here all the way to town.
Old Bill will come a trotting,
Tossing one after another down."

So as he plodded homeward
Can by can he laid a trail
Right back to the bar—
And he knew he wouldn't fail.

There he spied the pompous stranger
And he broke into a grin,
"Friend get out your thousand bucks,
For your wild man's coming in!"

"Now precautions have been taken,
For when Bill comes tippling in,
I don't want the town dogs
To drive him off again."

"So I've been to the big city pound,
Brought back a load of cats,
Told them I had a big old farm
That was overrun with rats."

"A boy I've got awaiting
Sitting atop a cage,
Inside are forty spittin' cats
Yowling out their rage."

"The town dogs are ringed about,
Putting on quite a show.
When he sees the wild man coming,
The boy'll let them damn cats go."

So when Bill reached the edge of town,
The boy flung the cage door open.
Forty cats went forty ways
Just as they'd been hopin'.

A hundred mutts in mad pursuit,
The cats made a wild retreat.
The coast was clear for old Bare-ass.
He came weavin' down the street.

The stage was set and ready
When Bill bounded through the door.
They leaped upon his naked back
And pinned him to the floor.

The stranger had him tightly bound,
Crated and boxed to go.
Said, "He'll be a big sensation,
The star of my side-show."

So old Bill sits within his cage,
And people come to stare,
To see him snarl and gnash his teeth
And greet them with a glare.

His disposition it is bad.
Hatred fills his mind.
A meaner specimen of man
It would be very hard to find.

So he sits and bares his fangs
And tosses his tangled mane.
He shakes his fist at passerbys
Who think him quite insane.

Who can blame the poor old guy,
His intentions were all good.
He set out into the hills
To do the best he could.

There he'd found a new life,
A rugged life but free.
He was tricked by Judas friends
Who wouldn't let him be.

He was trying to help his neighbors,
No wonder he's so teed.
For his friends they all forsook him
In their money craving greed.

Each day they toss Bill a hunk of meat,
All oozing blood and red.
They talk how he's much better off,
Housed and regular fed.

But old Bare-ass is not so happy.
He recalls the good old days.
If he could ever get aloose,
He'd go back to them ways.

Now there's a moral to this story,
One you should dwell upon—
"you can damn well get in trouble,
If you don't keep your britches on!"

Vaughn Short

Epilogue

So I've told my tale
I've spoke my words to you
Of raging river-lonely trail
Of misty mountain rising blue.

I hope I've caused a smile to be
Brought one chuckle or a grin
One small thought of breaking free
One old longing from within

At times I've sung a sad refrain
Sometimes with injustice burned
But my hopes were to entertain
As these pages you have turned.

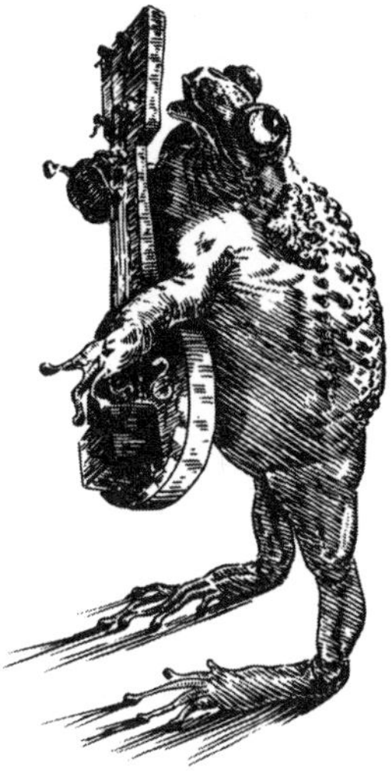

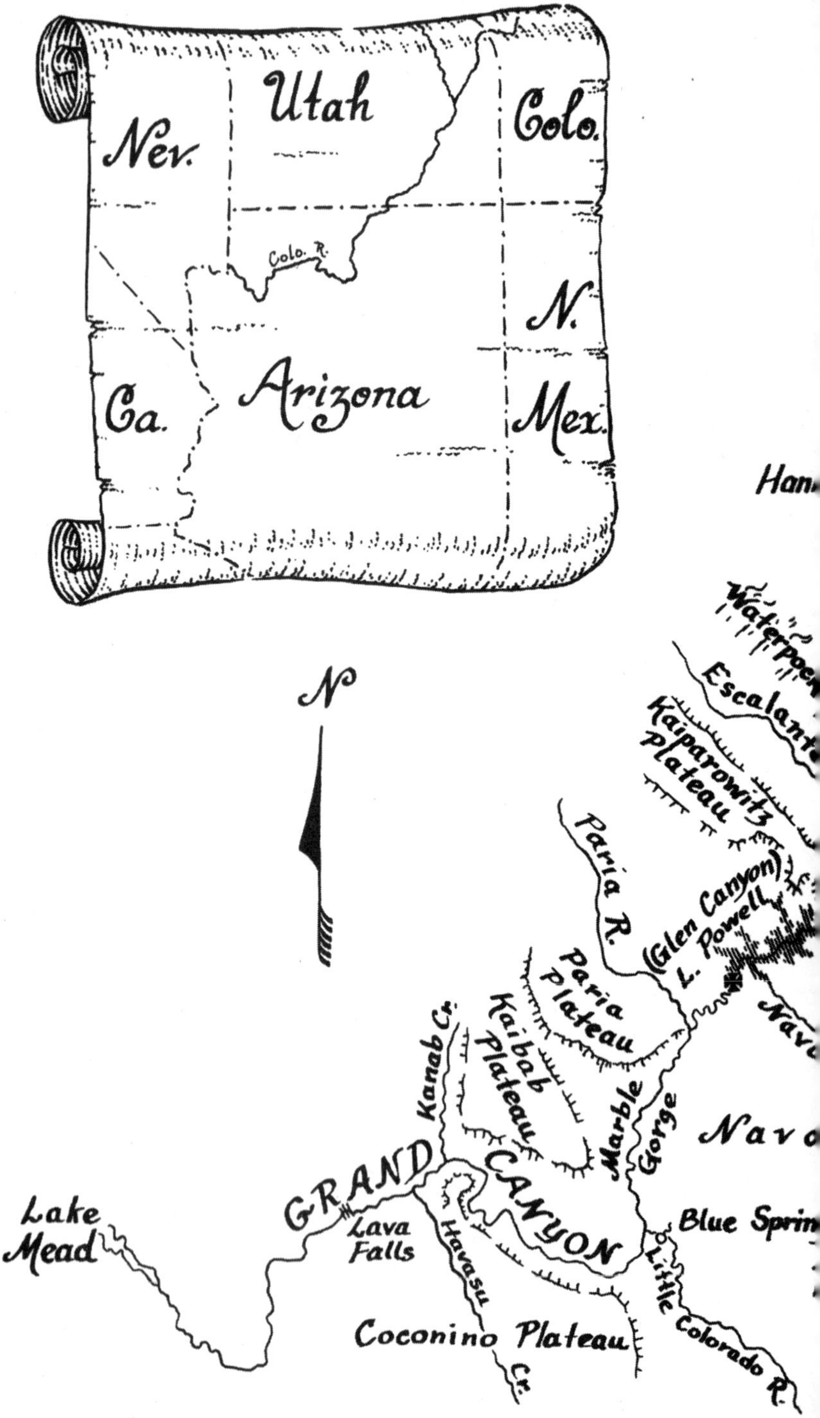
Utah
Nev.
Colo.
Colo. R.
N.
Mex.
Ca.
Arizona
N
Kaiparowits Plateau
Paria R.
(Glen Canyon)
L. Powell
Paria Plateau
Kaibab Plateau
Kanab Cr.
Marble
Gorge
GRAND
CANYON
Lake Mead
Lava Falls
Havasu
Cr.
Little Colorado R.
Coconino Plateau